Jones Beach

"John Hanc's history of Jones Beach is a delightful read, a nostalgic, absorbing trip back in time to the origins and the halcyon days of a treasured, New York institution. You can almost smell the cocoa butter!"

—*Kevin Baker, author of the best-selling New York-based trilogy* Dreamland, Paradise Alley *and* Strivers Row

"This is local history at its best. John Hanc's lively, absorbing narrative is both nostalgic and sophisticated, a love letter to a cherished playground of his youth and a social history of an important, innovative suburban recreation area. We taste the saltwater taffy and see the clean, orderly world of Jones Beach spread before us, planned by the autocratic Robert Moses, yet a public space that fulfilled the ideals of a great democracy. Hanc shows us how a beach came to embody the American dream."

—*Barnet Schecter, author of* The Battle for New York *and* The Devil's Own Work

Jones Beach

An Illustrated History

John Hanc

With a Foreword by Ed Lowe

Special Photography Courtesy of the Long Island Regional Archive,
New York State Office of Parks, Recreation and Historic Preservation

The Globe Pequot Press

GUILFORD, CONNECTICUT

The Globe Pequot Press is a division of Morris Book Publishing, LLC.

Photographs courtesy of the Long Island Regional Archive, New York State Office of Parks, Recreation and Historic Preservation, except for the following: page viii, courtesy Jane Reilly; p. xviii, courtesy Bob Harrison, New York State Parks, Long Island Region; pages 24, 29, 42–43, and 201, courtesy Daniel Goodrich; pages 32 and 44, courtesy of the Historical Society of the Massapequas; pages 46, 50, 51, 53, 152, and 183, courtesy of Bill Powell; page 97, courtesy Buymen Photos; and page 164, courtesy of Jay Lieberfarb.

Page 38: Prayer originally written in the Basque language by Joanes Etcheberri in 1627, English adaptation © Canadian Museum of Civilization, printed with permission.

Text design: Casey Shain

Library of Congress Cataloging-in-Publication Data
Hanc, John.
    Jones Beach : an illustrated history / John Hanc; with a foreword by Ed Lowe. — 1st ed.
        p. cm.
    Includes bibliographical references and index.
    ISBN-13: 978-0-7627-4024-6
    ISBN-10: 0-7627-4024-8
    1. Jones Beach State Park (N.Y.)—History. 2. Jones Beach State Park (N.Y.)—History—
Pictorial works. 3. Jones Beach State Park
(N.Y.)—Biography.   I. Title.
F127.N2H36 2007
974.7'245—dc22

                                                                        2006027198

Manufactured in China
First Edition/First Printing

Contents

Foreword

BY ED LOWE

Weekdays my childhood friends and neighbors gathered in the mornings at Amityville Village Beach, where we took swimming lessons and later dove into salt water 5 feet deep from a floating platform at the end of a pier that extended south from the beach.

The water was the Great South Bay, separating the South Shore of Long Island from the barrier islands that protected it from the Atlantic. At their roughest, the waves produced by the bay hit your body more as an annoyance than an adventure. The "real" beach was across the bay, across the barrier island, at the ocean.

If you didn't have a boat to take you directly south to Babylon Town's Gilgo Beach (and who did?) and you wanted to go to the real beach, you drove to Wantagh and took the parkway to the largest, oceanfront public bathing facility in the history of the world: Jones Beach State Park.

My next-door neighbors on Hamilton Street had a 1942 Ford sedan, faded maroon. It sputtered a little, and it always continued gasping and wheezing for a half minute after the driver turned the ignition to the off position. Five of their kids—plus me, and maybe one other boy from the block, with towels and a few plastic buckets and a picnic basket filled with jelly sandwiches wrapped in aluminum foil and some potato chips and

◄ *The crowded Central Mall area in 1957. Note the original flagpole to the right of the water tower.*

maybe some fruit—got wedged into that car on hot summer Saturday mornings. After the fashion of a sponge, the Wonder Bread always completely absorbed—subsumed—the Welch's grape jelly by the time anybody distributed the sandwiches later in the day, so they really weren't jelly sandwiches any more so much as matching pieces of jelly-flavored bread.

I don't know how we managed to fit into the Ford. I don't how we endured the heat inside, or the heat from outside, or from pressing, sweaty proximity to each other. I don't remember how far we walked—barefoot, probably—when we finally arrived, their father having parked the car way to the north of the Atlantic Ocean in one of the endless lots of Jones Beach State Park. I don't know how anybody kept everybody together when we returned to the car, hours and hours later, caked in ocean salt and basted with beach sand, our skin lobster red from the sun, our ears clogged, our brains exhausted from swimming, body surfing, tossing footballs,

▲ *Many families spent their summers at Jones Beach, including the Reilly family and friends, shown here in 1966.*

A 1950s view of the Central Mall area from the roof of the boardwalk refreshment stand. ▶

roaming, running, digging, arguing, and getting yelled at for getting lost or for getting sand on somebody's jelly bread.

But those are some of my first memories of Jones Beach; those and the panorama of endless sand and endless water, the endless boardwalk and the struggles to remove its inevitable splinters, the tastes of the Jones Beach hot dogs washed down with paper cups of cold cola, and the sweet saltwater taffy, which I believed was made with salt water, and the fresh water from the drinking fountains, and the cool, wet, sandy floor of the men's room at the main bathhouse, and the majestic staircase of the mammoth pool, whose center diving board, 10 feet high, I would not dare try until I was nine years old.

Wow. I've let that memory sit quietly by itself for a half century.

I jumped. Other kids were diving. I couldn't bear the thought of diving that far down, head first, or, worse, chest first.

However, after I accepted the challenge and climbed all the steps to the high diving board, and pulled myself up by the thick metal railings, I was there. Up there. I couldn't turn back, because . . . well, I couldn't. I was terrified. I couldn't turn. And, friends were watching me, and strangers. So, I couldn't turn back even if I could.

I walked slowly to the end of the board. Hundreds of people were in the pool below, far below, most of them swarming at the opposite end. I could see that they had left space for my body directly below me.

I closed my eyes, held my nose, and jumped.

I thought I never would hit the water. It took so long to arrive, I feared the rest of my party might have packed up and gone home without me. If I jumped on a Saturday, I didn't land until Sunday. Then I sank, and sank, and then swam to the surface, kicking, groping, arriving there on Monday, gasping for air, swimming madly for the pool perimeter, and swearing that I would never again approach the high board.

⚠ *Splashing and socializing in the refreshing West Bathhouse pool, 1950.*

I never did, never even approached the two lower boards. I embraced a disdain for the pool, saying, "Why would anybody waste their time in a stupid old pool, when the entire ocean was a short walk away?"

Funny that at sea level, at one of the flattest places on earth, you could learn so much about heights and your respect for them. With my parents I attended all the Guy Lombardo–produced shows at the Jones Beach Marine Theatre. On humid summer nights, I watched softball pitcher Eddie Feigner, known with his team as the "The King and His Court," as they humiliated whole other softball teams with an infield of three players, on the lighted softball fields at Jones Beach. I shot my first bow and arrow at a target at Jones Beach, listened there to live bands, and saw people dancing in the offshore evening breeze at a pavilion just north of the boardwalk. I played pitch 'n' putt golf for the first time at Jones Beach. I also got body slammed by a giant wave, rolled over and over in bruising sand mixed with abrasive shells, and thought for the first time that I was going to die in the surf at Jones Beach.

Three times, as a teen, I rode the utility bus west from Amityville to Wantagh, and then risked hitchhiking south on Wantagh State Parkway to Jones Beach, always worried that a New York State Parkway cop (long since merged with the New York State Police) would spot me before a generous motorist did. Twice, it was a parkway cop who picked me up and dropped me off at the central bathhouse. Both times officers warned me against the dangers of hitchhiking, said it was illegal, said I shouldn't do it, and gave me the ride anyway. Only a few years later, it seems, hitchhiking became *too* dangerous.

People who never have seen or experienced Jones Beach cannot know its significance to the generations who've found relief and relaxation there—and recreation, and rewarding employment, and lasting friendship, and romance, and contemplative peace and inspiration, and a repository for unparalleled memories of all that is good in a life, particularly a life lived on Long Island. Until now no one had ever written a real history of this vital part of Long Island life. I'm glad that John Hanc has done so—with words and pictures that tell the fascinating story of this place, so rich in memories . . . yours and mine.

Ed Lowe joined Newsday *as a reporter in 1969, and from 1976 until 2004 he was a columnist for the paper. Since 2005, he has been writing a weekly column for the* Long Island Press *and the* Neighbor Newspapers.

Introduction

The world has turned upside down. Reality has spun 180 degrees. At Jones Beach, 127,000 people have turned their backs to the ocean.

It's a scene rarely witnessed in three-quarters of a century of the beach's history. Typically, on a day like this—sunny, clear, in the seventies—the gaze is almost irresistibly drawn the other way, to an unbending, unending line of beach, water, sky. Out to the acres of sand so finely graded it appears as if each grain was turned by hand; across the greenish-blue waters, framed by the distant outlines of ships; and finally to a horizon and sky so impossibly vast that it prompts children on shore to squint out, hands cupped over their eyes, and declare, "Mommy, I think I can see England."

Overlooking the fact that if you sailed in a straight line from the beach you'd be headed not east to Europe but south to the Caribbean, such flights of fancy are understandable. Jones Beach State Park is located on the south shore of New York's Long Island, about 27 miles east of Manhattan. All of metropolitan New York and New Jersey's shorefronts have their charms, but only at Jones Beach does one get this sense of the unlimited. From the sprawling 6 miles of beaches to the spiraling towers of its art deco architecture, the sheer expanse of this colossal composition—recently and rightfully declared a historic landmark—is designed to demand full attention and endless possibility. Over the years Jones Beach has drawn praise from architects, municipal planners, historians, and editorial pages writers. Some of it suggests that the project is worthy of greater regard than as simply a place for a weekend's diversion. "Jones Beach speaks of a government dedicated to providing a truly noble public environment," *New York Times* architecture critic Paul Goldberger wrote. "It is a kind of people's palace."

For the people themselves—several generations of New Yorkers and visitors from all over the world—Jones Beach has provided the backdrop for warm summer memories. They know that you can come to Jones Beach to do many things, including not much of anything. But the one thing you cannot do is ignore it.

It would take something powerful to steal attention from this view. And on the Saturday of Memorial Day weekend 2005, the unofficial kick-off to the summer season, that something is about to appear. Whether spread out on blankets in bikinis or shorts, or huddled up in jackets and

⚠ *Packed parking lots on a crowded summer day.*

trousers on lawn chairs, this enormous crowd has turned to concentrate on one point: the Jones Beach water tower—itself worthy of sustained study, as it is the 231-foot beacon that has shown visitors the way here for nearly seventy-five years.

One could only hope that some would take this moment to notice the tower's intricate brick and stone work, its ornate peak, its Venetian stylings; that it might spark curiosity among them as to just how something straight out of the Italian Renaissance would have ended up here. At the center of this crowd, standing by a temporary two-story command center constructed on the boardwalk for this weekend, Sue Guliani looked around and smiled. This is something she does often, and not just because her job is to spend every day at the beach. Like most of the New York State parks employees who work here, Guliani has less connection with Albany than with the Atlantic. (Nor, it should be noted, does she have any connection with the famous, ex-New York City mayor of the same-sounding last name. However, when asked—which is often—she replies, "No relation, although I do have an Uncle Rudy.")

A native of Syosset, on Long Island's North Shore—the one facing the sound, not the ocean—she has her own Jones Beach memories, and they are quintessential. While she was growing up, her father Richard worked as an engineer at Sperry's, one of the many defense and aerospace companies that formed the backbone of Long Island's economy during the Cold War and that provided employment for those who had emigrated from New York City to the developments emerging from the potato fields after World War II. On spring, summer, and early fall afternoons, Richard Guliani, who worked an early shift at the Sperry plant in Lake Success, would get home at 3:40. He and his wife Dorothy would pack the kids—Sue and her brothers Rick and Robert—and the chicken dinners Dorothy had cooked that afternoon into the car, and off to Jones Beach they'd go.

At the West End ball field, the Guliani family would eat dinner and watch the Industrial League softball games, with the surf as the sound-track. The men playing in these leagues in the 1950s and 1960s were veterans of World War II and Korea; many were still in their prime, and at a time when baseball was king in America, they were the kings of the night at Jones Beach. Games were hard fought and action packed. Sue remembers what a perk it was to be allowed to keep score, which taught her the sport she would later play and coach, before her career took her back to the beach.

With a pager and cell phone clipped to her blue pants and a walkie-talkie in her hand, Sue, now the director of Jones Beach State Park, was in constant demand this day. Arriving at around 6:30 A.M., she found the beach already stirring with walkers and joggers, early sunbathers and visitors jockeying for position for the main event. For the past few hours, she'd been speaking with representatives from an alphabet soup full of agencies—DOT, FAA, DEC, State Parks, State Parks Police, Coast Guard—and still had time for a quick word and hug for her parents, Richard (now retired) and Dorothy, who continue to come to Jones Beach, proud now to say that it's their daughter who runs the place.

This was tricky business, months in the works, and it was all about to culminate. A woman wearing a headset leaned over and said, "In sixty seconds, they'll be over the tower." As ominous music swelled over the garish loudspeakers that had been strung up along the boardwalk, a man with a voice like a boxing announcer hyped up a moment that needed no hype, or music, for that matter. "Are . . . you . . . *rrrreadddyyyyyy, Long Island*?" he roared, as if about to introduce two heavyweights in a title bout.

One hundred and twenty seven thousand pairs of eyes searched the sky. Even the waves seemed to stop. And then . . . *whoosh*, there they were: three red, white, and blue missiles, streaking over the tower in formation, the United States Air Force Thunderbirds, the precision flying team that would provide the grand finale to the air show—officially called the Bethpage Federal Credit Union Air Show, a reminder of the beach's increasing dependence on outside sponsorship. The show had started at 10:00 A.M.; now, after four hours of World War I biplanes, World War II fighter planes, mock rescue missions by helicopters, stunt flying by F-15 jets, and precision parachute drops onto the beach by the Army's Golden Knights team, the show was finally reaching its climax.

The crowd cheered as the five F-16C jets—two others swept in from the west to join their mates—roared by at 1,200 miles per hour while Neil Diamond's "America" blasted over the speakers, loud enough to be heard over the jets, whose noise level was measured at 113 decibels.

The Long Island State Park Department came up with the idea of an air show to celebrate Jones Beach's seventy-fifth anniversary in 2004. It was a home run. "This place," said one parks official, "was made for this."

In one sense, he was right. The almost unlimited sight lines make it perfect for watching F-16s perform their rolls, loop-de-loops, and so-called knife's edge pass (in which two jets fly seemingly straight at each other, narrowly avoiding collision), and the 2-mile-long boardwalk and its benches, not to mention the beach itself, create an unparalleled viewing area.

The huge crowds on hand for the 2005 show were cause for celebration in part because, based on traffic patterns, these visitors seemed to be coming from Long Island, as well as New York City. This delighted park officials, who have long expressed concern and frustration over the declining attendance, especially from Nassau-Suffolk, the two suburban counties

△ *Jets soar into summer at the Jones Beach air show, 2006.*

of Long Island. "People tell me, 'I don't go there anymore,'" lamented George Gorman, a Long Island State Parks administrator. "I want to scream when I hear that! This is a treasure in your own backyard."

Indeed it is for me. Like Guliani and many other Long Islanders, Jones Beach figures into my earliest and some of my most precious memories. In my family, the attraction wasn't dinner and a ball game. My dad hated baseball, softball, or any variation of it. He was Czech, and like most Europeans, he preferred other sports. One was swimming, which he did often at Jones Beach. In the 1960s we would drive there from our home in Malverne, a little, bucolic village tucked into the already-overdeveloped western edge of Nassau County. I remember watching my dad from the water's edge, his arms periodically rising out of the water as he stroked far, far out, and then turned and came back to me.

He couldn't get enough of Jones Beach—and neither could my grandfather, who was able to leave Czechoslovakia and visit us on certain summers when the Communist authorities then in control of his country were feeling particularly charitable. I remember walking alongside them on the boardwalk on a brilliant summer day in 1966: my dad, then a fit and handsome man of forty-one; my erect, dignified grandfather, then in his early seventies, wearing a jaunty Jones Beach cap he'd bought from the souvenir shop on the boardwalk and puffing on a cigar. For them, this experience was nearly miraculous, and it wasn't until later that I figured out why. They had grown up in a landlocked country. The beach—and particularly *this* beach, with its vast expanses and that open-endedness—was on a scale they could have never imagined in old Prague's narrow, crooked streets.

Jones Beach and I continued on together. As a teenager hanging out with my friends at West End II, the "new" section of the beach that became a boomer haven in the 1960s and 1970s, I did a few things I shouldn't have, but had a lot of fun in the process. Later, as an uncertain twenty-five-year-old returning to Long Island after college and a few years working in Boston (where, I was shocked to find, you had to drive hours to find beaches even remotely as good as this), I drove down to Jones Beach on an unseasonably warm Sunday in March 1980. There, in the West End II parking lot, I struck up a conversation with a redheaded woman in a green Toyota. A year later we were married. Four years after that, we were divorced. The day she moved out, in May 1985, I ran a half-marathon footrace that started in Eisenhower Park in mid-Nassau County, headed 13 miles south, down the Wantagh Parkway, and finished on the Jones Beach boardwalk.

My relationship with the redhead started and ended there, but my love affair with Jones Beach continued hot and heavy. I have returned there as a reporter for *Newsday*, writing about various aspects of the beach over the years, including a summer-long series commemorating the seventy-fifth anniversary. I have returned there to mourn the loss of the father who loved the place as much as I did and as a happily remarried father myself, hoping to introduce my son to one of his dad's special places.

At the Memorial Day weekend air show, nine-year-old Andrew Hanc was more impressed by seeing Greg Biffle's #16 National Guard–sponsored NASCAR—one of the many special attractions held along the boardwalk that day as part of the air show—than he was with the grandeur of the beach. Perhaps such appreciation will develop as he gets older; perhaps not. Maybe, as some say, the days of large numbers of people coming to the beach for things other than air shows, fireworks displays, or concerts are gone. Jones Beach, after all, is not computerized. And the fact that it was used on this weekend as an open-air backdrop to what amounted to a live, giant-scale, reality TV show may be just a sign of the times.

Whatever it was, it worked: Attendance figures for the air show were the largest ever recorded during Memorial Day weekend at Jones Beach State Park. But the people who studied those numbers understood that there was also something slightly disheartening in the statistics. On the Saturday of that weekend, the first day of the air show, attendance was 127,000. On Sunday, again with the air show as the draw, 213,000 flocked to the beach, filling all six parking lots, and even parking along Ocean Highway, the road that connects the state park's beaches.

Memorial Day Monday, despite perfect weather again, a mere 41,000 showed up to enjoy Jones Beach without Thunderbirds and NASCAR.

Annual attendance at Jones Beach State Park is still about five million, far greater than any other attraction on Long Island and more than many things in adjacent New York City. Although that is a marked decline from its heyday in the thirty years or so following World War II, even on a hot Saturday in July in the early twenty-first century, Jones Beach is still a destination: The parking lots are filled, the parkways jammed, the concession stands packed, the sands at the main oceanfront beaches teeming.

But its vast expanses always seem able to accommodate. On the Saturday of the air show, out on Field Six, the easternmost of the park's oceanfront beaches, there was a sense that the beach was coming to life for yet another season, at its own pace, almost indifferent to the jets overhead and the hoopla further west on the boardwalk. The regulars were there: The Concretians is what they call the ones who sit in chairs on the concrete of the concession area; the Sandanistas are the ones who venture out and plant their blankets on the sand. They are generally older and more tanned than everyone else, and they have their memories of the beach, too, from the days when it and they were young.

Those days, and the ones before it—all the way back to the time when the beach was a remote sandspit on the edge of an empire—are the focus of this book.

CHAPTER 1

THE BATTLE
FOR THE BEACH

Swollen by decades of immigrants, New York in the first part of the twentieth century was a city of people living the Emma Lazarus line inscribed
on the Statue of Liberty. These "huddled masses yearning to breathe free,"
however, also yearned for freedom from the tyranny of the teeming street,
the overcrowded tenement, the densely packed subway car, the air fouled
by the emissions of the new motor vehicles and machines that powered
modern New York. Thanks to the advent of mass-produced, affordable
automobiles, many of these same people now had the means to escape, but
without a place to go.

A man named Robert Moses would construct the escape route.

Long Island, easily accessible and wide open, seemed a logical choice.
Development of parks on both its North and South shores—as well as a

◁ *Heading home on the Wantagh Parkway spur after a day at the beach, 1933.*

series of new roads to link them—became the centerpiece of the $15 million state parks expansion bill Governor Al Smith introduced in May 1924. In the weekly cabinet meetings, as discussions turned more and more toward the east, Smith—the "Happy Warrior," who had himself risen from the slums of the Lower East Side to become governor and a champion of the working man—would often reminisce fondly about "old" Long Island. He recalled times when as a younger man in the late nineteenth and early twentieth century, he would drive or ride out from the city, all the way east on a dirt road, and hardly encounter a traffic cop or stop light. Moses, an idealistic Yale graduate who had acquired a reputation as the brainiest of Smith's brain trust, owned a residence in Babylon on Suffolk County's South Shore. He had a more sophisticated and up-to-date understanding of Long Island than those who rarely ventured over the East River from Manhattan. Despite the prevailing view, prevalent even today in some circles, that everything east of the Queens border was a potato farm, Moses realized that Long Island was actually a complex maze of overlapping local entities and constituencies who would stand together to oppose him. This coalition of spectacularly wealthy landowners, proud farmers, suspicious baymen, and stubborn, sometimes parochial town governments would seek to block his efforts to use their island as the release valve for a city ready to burst.

So began what could be called the Battle of Jones Beach. It was fought on many fronts and used many weapons for a decade. And of course, it was not only Jones Beach that was at stake—it was an entire park system that would become, for decades, the envy of the country. In 1924 it was unclear who would take control of this land: the towns, the state, or private interests. One thing was clear—at least to the farsighted Moses—nearly from the beginning: Jones Beach would be the jewel of that crown, but it would be hard won.

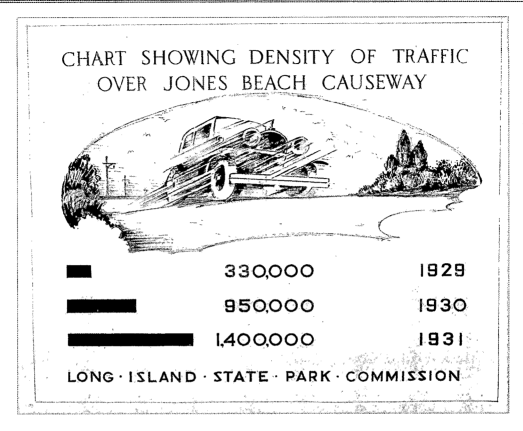

CHART SHOWING DENSITY OF TRAFFIC
OVER JONES BEACH CAUSEWAY

▬	330,000	1929
▬▬	950,000	1930
▬▬▬	1,400,000	1931

LONG · ISLAND · STATE · PARK · COMMISSION

▲ *Jones Beach attendance exploded in the early 1930s, as illustrated here.*

The First Traffic Jams

Nassau County in the 1920s was on the eve of a massive transformation that would culminate with the great post–World War II suburban boom. In some ways, however, it was still less like a growing New York City suburb and more like a remote district of western Pennsylvania or upstate New York. Towns were few and far between, families were large and intermarried. Entrenched attitudes, especially toward outsiders, were as hard and unwelcoming as the miserable, unpaved roads that snaked through its

△ *Five years prior to this photograph (taken in 1934), Jones Beach was a remote, isolated sandbar, accessible only by boat. The construction of the Wantagh and Southern State Parkways made the new state park possible.*

interior and along its coasts. With or without the looming presence of Moses, pressure on the county to modernize was mounting in many ways. The population was increasing, from 126,120 residents in 1920 to 303,053 in 1930. With it came increased traffic, some of it from residents (the number of registered vehicles in Nassau soared from 40,000 in 1922 to more than 112,000 by 1930). But much of the volume came from city dwellers. In a single-hour period on August 20, 1922, 1,687 cars were counted on Merrick Road in Rockville Centre. Most of these were families who sought relief from the city for a day.

They found none on their journey through Long Island.

" 'The day in the country' consists of riding in a steady stream of automobiles along a road, both sides of which is bordered by private property bearing the words 'No Trespassing,'" wrote one local legislator, in support of Smith's bill.

Things were even worse in 1924. At the time that Moses was beginning the fight to build the state roads and parks that would transform the region, the Ku Klux Klan was active on Long Island, part of that odious organization's national resurgence throughout the country during that decade. In August the Klan held a rally in Hempstead attended by 600 people. That was followed a month later, with a march by 700 Klansmen and supporters in Freeport. There were Klan organizations in Valley Stream, Farmingdale, and other communities as well. The Klan of Long Island in the 1920s was not as violent or overt in its hatred as, say, the Klan of the Deep South during the 1950s and 1960s; in fact, owing to the paucity of African Americans on Long Island, the local Klan primarily turned its hatred toward Jews and Italians instead. In subsequent decades when Moses—who was Jewish—spoke of the difficulties faced in the creation of Jones Beach and his other state parks, he often made a point of mentioning the Klan as one of the obstacles he faced. In one magazine story printed years later, it was claimed that he led a gang of "huskies" and smashed up a bathhouse owned by an influential local Klan leader and politician, who had refused to move off of Jones Beach. Given the Klan's minimal impact during its dramatic but brief resurgence on Long Island— not to mention the fact that there is no mention anywhere of a bathhouse existing on Jones Island, outside of the small summer colony known as High Hill Beach, before 1929—that's probably a bit of an overstatement. "Moses liked to paint his opponents with as much tar as he could," says county historian Edward J. Smits. "Many of the people active in community life at the time may have been Klan members, but there was no evidence that they were rallying against his proposals."

◬ *The fun didn't stop once the sun set: Dancing before the band shell, 1934.*

The Locals Resist

Moses's biggest obstacle in the development of Jones Beach was most likely
the solid, if suspicious, citizens of the towns of Babylon, Oyster Bay, and
Hempstead. In 1924 the newly formed Long Island State Park
Commission, chaired by Moses, attempted to secure Jones Island, which,
typical of the fragmented dividing lines of Long Island, stretched across two
counties and three townships. Moses was rebuffed by the Town of Babylon
(in Suffolk County) and then by the Town of Oyster Bay in Nassau (which

▲ *Jones Beach was known for its clean and tidy appearance.*
Note the uniformed sweepers at center.

was already up in arms about his plans to build parks and parkway on the
North Shore). "It is a ridiculous situation," said Babylon Assemblyman John
Boyle in a meeting with Moses present. "They are here to make plans for
all of us on Long Island. We don't want that. We don't want people coming in and telling us where we shall have parks, when there is no public
demand for them."

In a letter to a friend in Babylon, Moses acknowledged that he was
"disgusted" with Boyle, who had helped draft a Suffolk County resolution
opposing the creation of the new State Park Commission. But Moses
seemed to dismiss his efforts as inconsequential. "We will pass the bill, anyway," he said.

While the State Park Commission was indeed created, the issue of securing the land to create the parks was another matter. It seemed that the sentiments of Boyle and like-minded Long Islanders would prevail when, in a referendum on election day 1925, voters of the Town of Hempstead in Nassau County were asked whether they wanted to turn over their 5-mile strip of land on Jones Beach and part of what was then called Short Beach, just west of it, to the state for the purposes of developing a state park. The voters said "no" by a count of 12,106 to 4,200.

The Hempstead vote crushed Moses. "It looked like we'd lost Jones Beach," he told biographer Robert Caro years later. "It looked absolutely hopeless."

Hope came in a rather unlikely form: Republican assemblyman Tom McWhinney of Lawrence and the powerful Town of Hempstead Republican boss G. Wilbur Doughty. These two men were born during the Civil War, grew up when Long Island was still a rural backwater, and emerged as important local Republican leaders when Nassau County was formed at the turn of the century.

At the urgings of McWhinney—a man who, Moses said, "grasped the scope" of what he was proposing—Doughty agreed to meet with the commissioner after the failed referendum. The portly, walrus-mustachioed boss would later admit—in front of several thousand people at the opening of Jones Beach State Park—that he thought the whole project was "a pipe dream." In the meeting with Moses and McWhinney, Doughty began to see the possibilities of what Moses was proposing. Still, as political boss, he had a job to do. In what appears to be a classic back-room deal, Doughty gave his support for Jones Beach. What he got out of it, Caro suggests, was a construction contract on the project for his brother-in-law's firm.

Victory at Last

A year later, November 1926, the referendum was on the bill again in the Town of Hempstead. In a stunning change of heart—or collective twist of arm—the citizens overwhelmingly supported the bill to give Jones Beach to the state.

Not long after, the *New York Times* was applauding the Town of Hempstead for "carrying forward its good work in behalf of state parks."

Moses wasted no time in getting to that work. A month after the referendum passed, the first engineering stake was driven into the sands of Jones Beach at the precise spot where the water tower now stands. Construction began shortly afterward on a causeway—400 feet wide and almost 5 miles long—that would link the beach to the mainland of Long Island. Its projected cost: $400,000. In its editorial of January 3, 1927, the *Times* noted that opposition to the plan was still widespread from many corners and dismissed the critics:

> The main facts are simple—that Jones Beach is an ideal spot for recreation, with excellent bathing facilities in surf and still water, exposed to the cool southerly breezes during the Summer months and rich in picturesque dunes and camp sites. The State now has the opportunity to push work on what promises to be one of the finest and most useful recreation grounds near New York City.

To those who continued to resist the efforts of Moses and his Long Island State Park Commission, the *Times*—an unwavering supporter of the project throughout the 1920s—had this to say: "Long Islanders who try to check the influx of motorists and picnickers apparently do not realize that they are fighting against a resistless avalanche."

Some would say that avalanche had a name: Bob Moses.

▲ *Aerial view of Jones Beach State Park on July 3, 1938.*

"The job we had," Moses said later, "was to recapture for the people a part of the ocean front, most of which was in the hands of private owners." Although that was really not the case at Jones Beach—most of the beach was in public, not private hands—his bellicose language shows the zeal with which this self-appointed warrior for the people attacked the problem. At stake was his vision for the new state park: a vision based in the idealism of his mentor Smith and Moses's own belief in the power of government to further the best interests of the people (sometimes whether the people were interested or not), and rooted in his contempt for what he saw as selfish private interests and squandered opportunities, exemplified by Coney Island.

By the time construction began on Jones Beach, Coney Island had already been a flourishing seaside resort for almost half a century. It was world famous, it was enormous, it was crowded . . . and, to Moses, it was disgusting: dirty, tawdry, filled with cheap amusements and low entertainments that brought out the worst in human nature. There was nothing edifying in Coney Island, as far as he was concerned. He saw it as a once-beautiful ocean beachfront, exploited by greed and ultimately wasted. "Every square inch of the precious shore was preempted by speculators who had one ambition, to cash in and get away," Moses wrote. Nor was he enamored with Rockaway or Long Beach, just to the west of Jones Beach, where the only things separating private development and the ocean were narrow ribbons of beach and boardwalk. Moses had a better idea, which he articulated in a speech twenty years later: "The first intelligent barrier beach plan was made by the State at Jones Beach, where there were no speculators to conciliate, and no catchpenny operators and politicians to fix."

As the plan he referred to was his, Moses was essentially saying "I am the state." This would have been hard to argue given the influence that he wielded during this period, "a power so substantial," Caro would later write, "that it was not challenged seriously by any Governor of New York State . . . during a 34-year period."

Still, Moses's claims about no special interests to deal with were not entirely true. He was fighting—and conciliating—on many fronts in the late 1920s, even as the work on the beach proceeded. On election day in 1927—one year after the decisive Hempstead referendum—voters of the Town of Oyster Bay ceded their part of Jones Beach to the state, which included High Hill Beach. Later, the Town of Babylon conveyed additional land. Still, there was resistance. The *Saturday Evening Post*'s Edmond Fish wrote:

> Over a period of three years, Moses hurdled real estate title obstacles and galloped through a broken field of would-be tacklers—state, county, city and town politicians. He campaigned through town and village, speaking at meetings and taking tea with ladies' clubs. There were referendums to be won. Battle lines reached from Long Island town halls to the capitol in Albany . . . lawsuits broke like waves on the shoreline.

In one of these lawsuits, the Seaman-Gore case, heirs of John Seaman invoked royal land grants dating back to the 1600s to block the state's claim to parts of the beach. The case dragged on for ten years and ended up in the U.S. Supreme Court, which ruled in favor of the state. All the while construction of the new state park—Moses promised it would be "a miracle playground for the public"—continued. It was based on a simple if monumental plan. A new road to the park—a "parkway"—from New York would be constructed, running east through unused lands originally purchased by the city's water development authority. In Wantagh, on Nassau County's South Shore, the parkway would link with another new road; this one would be constructed over the marshes of South Oyster Bay and would lead directly to the beach. "That was the idea behind Jones Beach and the Southern State Parkway," Moses told Caro. "I thought of it all in a moment."

The Long Road

The inspiration may have come in a flash, but the building of the new state park and its connecting roads would be undertaken in long, arduous phases. The first objective was to reach the beach. Over the winter of 1926, construction crews on the new Jones Beach Causeway proceeded relentlessly south, like an army building its roads ahead of itself, marching through the marshy wilderness. And, like most armies, they ran into trouble. Labor strikes temporarily stopped all work at one point, and one of the causeway contractors, a company based in New Jersey, went broke. When the remaining contractors were unable to borrow enough funds to continue, Moses borrowed $20,000 from his mother (heiress of a real estate fortune) to help the effort.

While the causeway was moving south, another construction project was under way. What was called "one of the biggest dredging jobs in America" lifted 40,000,000 cubic yards of sand from the bottom of South Oyster Bay and dumped it along the barrier beach, giving it a midline altitude of 14 feet above sea level and effectively protecting it from being swamped by heavy seas ever since. The dredging job—which also created the State Boat Channel across the bay—was not without hazards. During the operation, the engineering crew camped out on the marshy reefs in the bay. For one ten-day period, they were marooned when ice packs choked off boat access in the bay. A decade later, Sid Shapiro, who became one of Moses's top deputies but was then part of the dredging crew,

▲ *Grooming the sand for the construction of the boardwalk near the East Bathhouse, 1933.*

recalled the experience. "We had plenty of pancake flour and very little else towards the end of ten days. I still can't eat pancakes even now."

Back on the beach itself, the first structure in the new state park was being planned, located on the site of a natural inlet that had closed naturally—and conveniently for Moses—in the mid-1920s. The new building would be strategically located so that bathers could have easy access to the ocean on one side and Zach's Bay on the other. Moses wanted this building to make a statement: that Jones Beach was going to be very different than any other beachfront park or resort, anywhere. It was an expensive statement. The $150,000 appropriation of funds by the state legislature for what would become known as the East Bathhouse was sufficient only to construct the foundation. The legislators had heard "bathhouse" and

△ The grand East Bathhouse in 1935.
▽ Charming silhouetted signs point the way to some of the many facilities
to be found at the East Bathhouse.

envisioned the kind of wooden pavilions that had been common in beach resorts for a century (a particularly rickety example of which stood barely a mile east at High Hill Beach.) Moses wanted no part of that. Just as they would later do when he presented his idea of a water tower, the legislature balked.

"Trouble was," Moses said contemptuously, "those boys just couldn't see anything bigger than a hat rack."

In a sense, who could blame them? Before the construction of the East Bathhouse, "changing rooms were small wooden cabins . . . cramped, mildewy, sandy," says beach historian and author Lena Lencek. "Jones's grandiose bathhouse marked a critical advance in the process of democratizing the beach, of bringing the benefits of the seaside within comfortable reach of the masses."

The new bathhouse had 10,450 lockers and dressing rooms, a mini-hospital, a snack bar, and stations for umbrella rentals (50 cents a day). With its rusticated Ohio sandstone, sundeck, time and tide dials, and other details (such as sidewalk mosaics of a compass and seahorse), it would also be an aesthetic triumph, the first of many on Jones Beach.

On yet another front, the Southern State Parkway was being completed. Once ready, New Yorkers could drive all the way from the city, almost 30 miles away, to the new Jones Beach State Park with no stoplights or crossing grades—and not a NO TRESPASSING sign to be found.

Ready to Go

By the spring of 1929, everything was near readiness: The 4½-mile-long causeway began at the intersection of Merrick Road in Wantagh and would be connected from the north by Wantagh Parkway, which linked to Southern State Parkway (and eventually to the Northern State Parkway that was, at that moment, another bone of contention between Moses and local government and landowners). The causeway spanned three new bridges to connect Jones Beach to the mainland: The Island Creek Bridge was 100 feet long; the Sloop Channel Bridge, 878 feet long; and the Goose Creek "lift" (draw) bridge, 521 feet long. All three were a uniform 74 feet in width. At the beach the causeway linked to a plaza, still under construction, at the center of which would rise an enormous tower, flanked by reflecting pools. Through the plaza ran a new road bisecting Jones Island. The Ocean Boulevard, as it was called at that point, was 40 feet wide and 3 miles long.

Just southeast of that plaza stood the new, expensive bathhouse, funds for which had eventually—if reluctantly—been pried from the State Assembly. As promised, it looked nothing like a wooden beach pavilion. "It rose out of the landscape," says Matthew Dockery, an architecture and design professor at the New York Institute of Technology, "almost as if it was part of the beach. It looked like a force of nature."

It was not the power of nature but the potential of profit that caught the attention of the *New York Herald Tribune*. The paper, which had earlier editorialized in favor of local Long Island interests against the state, covered the imminent opening of the beach as a business story. Indeed, it's interesting to note that in both the August 4 and 5 (1929) editions of the paper, the opening of Jones Beach is not mentioned on its front page or even in its local news summary. All coverage was relegated to the business section. "The beach development, for which there is a crying need," noted one story, "will attract a great many thousands of visitors who heretofore have never visited this part of Long Island and naturally a great many will doubtless respond to the visible advantages of living near the causeway or investing in realty in this causeway zone for which there will unquestionably be a great demand."

△ *With its time and tide dials on opposite towers, the East Bathhouse rose "like a force of nature."*

In retrospect, although a stunningly narrow view of its significance, Jones Beach was seen as a potential boon to real estate at the time. In the weeks before the August 4 opening, advertisements had begun appearing in New York area newspapers offering houses and lots in new developments in Amityville, Freeport, Wantagh, and Massapequa Park, all touting their proximity to the new state park.

"Act Now!" read an ad for a new Tudor home (priced at $10,600) in the development known as Merrick Gables. "This summer a 10 minute auto ride will take you over the new Jones Beach Causeway to one of the most beautiful sand beaches on the Atlantic front."

"Next Sunday, when you attend the formal opening of the Jones Beach Causeway, visit us in Massapequa Park!" read another. "The Heart of the Sunrise Homeland."

"There is Only one Garden Gate to Jones Beach!" crowed yet another ad, this one for a business development known as Sunrise Park in Wantagh. "The State of New York has restricted its park-like road frontage against business. Sunrise Park is all business lots. Think what this means to the Speculator and Business Man today; then consider what it should mean when Jones Beach becomes one of the GREATEST OCEANFRONT PLAYGROUNDS IN THE WORLD."

That moment was at hand. At 2:00 P.M. on August 4, 1929, Jones Beach State Park was officially open to the public.

The ceremony for the new state park took place at the new bathhouse—located a little more than 27 miles east of the corner of 34th Street and 5th Avenue in midtown Manhattan. There, seven months later, another titanic symbol of the age, the Empire State Building, would soon begin to rise. The newly elected chairman of the corporation that would manage the construction of the new skyscraper was none other than Alfred E. Smith, the former New York state governor who had lost his bid for the U.S. presidency the previous year to Herbert Hoover, and who, on this day, sat on the dais at Jones Beach with his forty-year-old protégé, Robert Moses.

It was a proud day for both men. The parks bill, biographer Christopher Finan noted, would rank as one of Al Smith's greatest achievements as governor. When he took office in 1922, there were few state parks any-

△ *Gov. Franklin Delano Roosevelt speaking at the opening of Jones Beach State Park, August 4, 1929. Former Gov. Al Smith is seated to his left, and Robert Moses (in bow tie) is at far right.*

where in New York, outside of the forest preserves of the Adirondacks and Catskills. By the time he left six years later, the system had grown to seventy parks with more than 125,000 acres—9,700 of which were on Long Island—all linked by modern new parkways.

Down one of those parkways, the new Jones Beach Causeway, drove the cars of the powerful and the curious—on August 4. They parked in brand-new parking fields and walked along brand-new promenades that led them to a tent outside the first completed structure in the Jones Beach State Park. There, in the early afternoon, about 3,000 visitors (out of a total of 10,000 who visited the beach over the course of the day) gathered to listen to Smith; his successor as New York State governor, Franklin D. Roosevelt; Moses; and two local politicians who had played key roles in making Smith and Moses's dream a reality: Tom McWhinney, by then a Long Island State Park commissioner, and Hempstead town boss G. Wilbur Doughty, a Republican on a mostly Democratic stage. (Sadly, neither of these two men—without whom Jones Beach would never have succeeded—lived to see the new state park reach its true fruition: Doughty died in 1930, a year after the beach opened. McWhinney died in 1933.)

The memory of many of those in attendance at the beach's Opening Day was that of a sandstorm that blew across the beach, clogging up carburetors, stalling cars, and irritating guests. (To help prevent it from happening again, clumps of grass were later planted across the beach, anchoring the sand.) It's interesting that the sandstorm was barely mentioned in the news accounts that day. There was a larger story here—a story about what determined, well-intentioned government could do on behalf of its citizens. "It behooves us to give the people the benefits of what the State has to offer," Smith said in his remarks to the crowd. "The preservation of the health of the people is a vital concern. No State can rise above the physical strength of its people." To some, this—and indeed, the entire Jones Beach project—smacked of socialism. If so, Roosevelt said—no doubt with the patrician tone and broad smile that would soon become familiar to the entire nation—if Jones Beach and the new state park system were "socialistic," as some contended, "well, Governor Smith and I are pretty good socialists."

For Smith, "the Happy Warrior," the battle of Jones Beach was won. For Robert Moses, a somewhat less jovial combatant, the work was just beginning.

△ *Former Gov. Al Smith cuts the beach's anniversary cake while*
Robert Moses (in white suit) looks on, July 19, 1939.

The world would soon come to know the obscure barrier beach off
the south shore of Long Island, and Smith and Moses would be the men
most associated with its success. Few then and now, however, would know
the story of the remarkable man for whom the beach was named and that
of the little beach colony whose peaceful existence was about to come to
an end.

Here Lyes Inter'd The Body of
Major Thomas Iones Who Came From
Strabane In The Kingdom of
Ireland Settled Here And Died
December 715 From Distant Lands
To This Wild Waste He Came
This Seat He Choose And Here
He Fixd His Name Long May His
This Peace Full

CHAPTER 2

PIRATE JONES

At about 10:00 on the morning of July 1, 1690, William of Orange's army charged across the Boyne River, 30 miles from Dublin. On the opposite bank, the followers of the deposed King James II awaited them.

The ensuing battle, part of what would later become known as the Glorious Revolution, would help decide nothing less than the throne of England, Scotland, and Ireland for the next century. The international cast of combatants included French dukes, English lords, Hanoverian marshals—as well as a young Irish officer, Major Thomas Jones.

Born to a family of Welsh descent in Strabane, in County Tyrone, 150 miles north of Dublin, Jones was then about twenty-five years old. Little is known of his early life or exactly what happened to him in what would become known as the Battle of Boyne. Although one later historian

◁ *Grave of "pirate" Thomas Jones, Massapequa, New York.*

referred to Major Jones as "hero of the Boyne," more likely he was nothing more or less than a young, inexperienced officer in the army of untried Irish foot soldiers who made up the bulk of the Jacobites (as the followers of James were called).

William, who was Dutch and a Protestant, enjoyed the support of Parliament and much of Europe. James, a Catholic (and William's father-in-law) was backed by France, as well as many in Ireland, who saw in his victory an opportunity for independence from oppressive English rule. In the battle the Prince of Orange's Dutch-English army of 36,000 prevailed over the Jacobites, who numbered 21,000. When the Irish were finally outflanked by William's cavalry, they broke and ran—none faster than James, who kept going all the way to Dublin ahead of his retreating army. Once there, he blamed his defeat on his Irish soldiers—many of whom were among the 2,000 men killed in the battle—before sailing off to France, where he would spend the last eleven years of his life.

The battered army he left behind—Major Jones included—would fight on for another year and a half, culminating in the siege of the city of Limerick in 1692. There, a treaty was negotiated with King William, the terms of which included a provision for the Jacobite soldiers to leave Ireland to fight as mercenaries in other European armies. This mass exile by what has been estimated as 11,000 Irish became known as the Flight of the Wild Geese and is the subject of many a sad poem and ballad in Ireland to this day.

"Some nursed a romantic notion that they would, one day, return to fight for" Ireland, wrote historians Peter and Fionna Somerset Fry. "Others sought more realistically for adventure and fulfillment in foreign lands."

Leaving Ireland for the New World

Thomas Jones was one of the Wild Geese, and his flight would indeed lead him to adventure and fulfillment—and all the way to a desolate barrier beach in a new world on the other side of the ocean.

What would happen to this obscure young Irish officer between the time he left his native Ireland for good in 1692 and his death twenty-one years later in the New World was a life that could have seemingly been imagined only by a novelist or screenwriter. It's a story of swashbuckling derring-do on the high seas, narrow escapes from death, an improbable love affair, ascension to respectable high society, material success, and, finally, a ghoulish postmortem, tinged with tales of the supernatural. Not to mention a legacy that lives on in the form of a beach that bears his name and is known worldwide—although the man behind the name is largely forgotten.

The events that transpired right after the surrender of the Irish we have in Jones's own words from testimony given a few years later: "We were conveyed to France with our arms, brass guns and ammunition and that being thus conveyed continued to act under King James II, as our King, and were commissioned . . . as privateers."

Thomas Jones had become a pirate.

Pirate or privateer? Although some of his respectable descendants would try very hard to prove that he was the latter, the truth is that the two were often indistinguishable. According to British maritime historian David Cordingly, a pirate was (and is) defined as someone who robs and plunders on the sea. The word *privateer* referred to an armed vessel (or the commander of the vessel) that was licensed to attach and seize the vessels of a hostile nation. In the turbulent European political waters of the late seventeenth century, privateers were, in effect, an inexpensive method of harassing enemy shipping—a sort of outsourced navy, to use twenty-first-century terms. However, as Cordingly notes, "the system was wide open to abuse and privateers were often no more than licensed pirates."

Privateer Jones

Jones sailed under such a license—a letter of marque—in 1692. How he went from being an exiled soldier in a defeated army one day to commanding a ship with license to roam and plunder the seven seas the next, no one seems to know. But it suggests that Jones was a man of rare qualities, a persuasive fellow, and a born leader, whose talents manifested themselves not in sleepy Irish shires but in the pirate-infested waters of the Spanish Main, which is where Jones found himself, hunting Spanish ships in the Caribbean as part of the ongoing profitable campaign being waged against the treasure galleons of Spain.

This was the golden age of piracy, and Jones was apparently right in the middle of it—at least until he was captured by the English in circumstances unknown. In 1693 Thomas Jones and seven other Irishmen stood trial for piracy in London. The proceedings, printed in an old English law report, even record his testimony, in which he claims that "the ship and goods we took by virtue of a commission as privateers, and that therefore we ought to be treated as only enemies and prisoners of war." Supposedly, King William himself ordered the trial, which showed the lingering bitterness over those who had sided with his rival—James—during the still-recent campaign in Ireland and in what had gone on to explode into a European conflict known as the Nine Years War. There was apparently insufficient evidence to convict Jones. The record of this trial, discovered by family historian John H. Jones in the late nineteenth century, is one of the only recorded traces we have of Jones's early years. No likeness of the

▲ *Parts of Long Island look very much as it did when the Quakers arrived in the 1600s.*

man, at any point in his life, exists (an early-nineteenth-century painting, supposedly of Thomas Jones, hanging in the main offices of Jones Beach State Park is actually that of a descendant). Although most pirate captains were neither the clean-cut swashbucklers portrayed by Hollywood or the loveable rogues of Gilbert and Sullivan, Jones does seems to have been a bit of both. "I think he had to be dashing and charming in order to achieve what he did," says Lillian Bryson of the DeLancey Floyd-Jones Library.

Privateers didn't advertise their movements, so tracing Jones at this point in his life is difficult. There are accounts of him sailing as far as Madagascar—a pirate haven—and then back halfway around the world to Rhode Island, where he become linked to Thomas Townsend, the man who changed his life and helped propel Jones to the status to which Bryson alludes. Townsend was a Quaker and a scion of what, even in the late seventeenth century, would have been considered an established family in North America. His father, John, had arrived in Boston in 1637 and soon emigrated south to Flushing, a village on what was the Dutch-ruled western end of Long Island. As the English began to push south from New England, conflicts between the two nations arose, many of them centered on the fish-shaped island—extending 120 miles east from Manhattan—that had been discovered by Dutch skipper Adrian Block.

Somewhere in the mid-1600s, John Townsend and his two brothers moved east to a new settlement known as Oyster Bay, on the north shore of what is today Nassau County. His conflicts with the Dutch over religion and politics continued—at one point, Townsend was summoned by governor Peter Stuyvesant to appear before him in New Amsterdam, presumably for a firm tongue lashing—but as their influence waned on Long Island, the Townsends not only survived but thrived, eventually becoming prominent citizens and wealthy landholders, whose interests stretched beyond Oyster Bay.

Rhode Island was not only friendly to Quakers, it was also located on the other end of the Long Island Sound—a major highway in an era when commerce was conducted mostly via water. Merchants would often send a family member to oversee their trade interests at the other end of the "highway," which is probably why Thomas Townsend—son of John— was in Portsmouth, Rhode Island, the day a certain Thomas Jones arrived. In addition to having close commercial and family ties, the coastal towns of Rhode Island and Long Island were known to be tolerant of—if not actively involved in—the pirate trade. Thomas Townsend himself was once remonstrated for allowing a convicted pirate to escape jail while he was sheriff. So it is entirely possible that he may have financed Jones on some of his later voyages as a privateer. Or it could have been that after several close shaves with death—not to mention a new get-tough policy on pirates that was instituted by the English during the Nine Years War—Jones realized that the buccaneer bubble had burst and decided it was time for a career change.

The Pirate and the Merchant

What is clear is that the two men—the Quaker merchant (about fifty years old when he met Jones) and the Irish privateer (who was by that time about thirty)—became friends and business partners. Townsend, described as a "man of untiring energy" and "a beloved and trusty friend," was all that and more to the younger Jones. The bond became especially close when, in 1695, Jones married Townsend's twenty-year-old daughter, Freelove. Thomas Townsend himself, a justice of the peace, is said to have presided over the ceremony.

Thomas Townsend was also rich. In 1693 he purchased about 6,000 acres on what is now the South Shore of eastern Nassau County from the local Indians for about fifteen pounds. Townsend also owned land in the village of Oyster Bay, as well as a house, built in 1660, that he gave to Thomas and Freelove in 1696. There was more good news to come: On June 29, 1696, Thomas Townsend gave Jones and Freelove 300 acres of his land on Fort Neck. In the deed Townsend wrote that the land was being given "in consideration of my natural love and affection to Thomas Jones, my son-in-law."

The land was on a peninsula—called Fort Neck, because it was believed to be the site of an earlier Indian fortification—amidst the salt meadows of the South Oyster Bay, a large body of water located on the

▲ *A painting of the Oyster Bay house where Thomas and Freelove Jones lived.*

south coast of Long Island between the mainland and the long string of barrier beaches on the Atlantic. It was there, after about a year in the village of Oyster Bay, that the new lord of the manor and his wife built their castle. Erected alongside a creek, Jones's house was constructed of brick, with a gabled pitched roof and chimneys on each gable. It was one of the first and most substantial homes built on this part of Long Island, which, if not quite a howling wilderness, was still a remote outpost in the New World. One story holds that before Jones came on the scene, Thomas Townsend had offered this same land to his son, John. Horrified at the prospect of living in the swamps of Long Island's south shore, he is supposed to have retorted, "Does my father want me to go out of the world?"

The well-traveled Jones had no such reservations. Working from this remote base, he would begin his own rise as a citizen in polite society—a spectacular and well-documented ascent, especially considering his vague, Jolly-Rogered past. Using what must have been a powerful personal charm and magnetism, he seems to have befriended almost everyone, from the local Indians to the royal governors. Very telling is Jones's involvement in organized religion. One ancestral historian insisted that the major was a "staunch" Anglican, and in 1703 he was indeed elected warden of the established Anglican Church in Oyster Bay; later, he held the same position at a church in the neighboring town of Hempstead. This is a man who had fought for a Catholic king and married into a Quaker family.

He was ambitious, opportunistic, entrepreneurial—an American success story before there really was an America. Although he seemed to demonstrate the egalitarian streak that was common among privateer ships of that era—when captains were elected and the crews were often racially mixed—Jones himself became a slaveholder (in fact, as late as the early 1900s, many African Americans with the surname Jones, descendants of the major's slaves, were still living in the Massapequa area).

The roguish Jones also exhibited tenderness and a concern for the public good—at least according to one of the stories handed down through the family. Supposedly, he and Freelove once traveled from Fort Neck to some of the Townsend-Jones family land in Cold Spring Harbor, near Oyster Bay. It was a long ride by cart, and at one point, Freelove expressed her thirst and suggested they stop at a nearby stream. Major Jones told her to wait; he knew of better water ahead. On reaching that spot he sprang out of the cart, walked over to the spring, filled his hat up with water, and brought it back to her. Having slaked her, his, and their horse's thirst with cold, clear water from the spring, Jones remarked to his wife, "I shall give this stream to the town for a water place forever." He kept his promise, and as of 1900—when this story was set down on paper by a descendant—the place was still known as a public watering place, or "the Spout."

Trader Jones

Jones could afford such generosity. The man exiled from his native land had risen rapidly in his adopted one. First, working with his father-in-law, Jones set out to acquire more land, and through trading with the local Indians eventually amassed 4,700 additional acres throughout what is now the South Shore of Nassau County (it's worth noting that Jones, again perhaps as a result of his years dealing with the ethnically and racially mixed crews of privateers, was said to be very friendly and fair in his dealings with the natives). In 1702 he was appointed captain (later major) of the Queens County Militia; in 1703 he was elected church warden; in 1704 he was appointed high sheriff of Queens County (essentially the highest law enforcement official in the county); and in 1710 the royal governor of New York appointed Thomas Jones the ranger-general of the island of Nassau (the English name for Long Island). As ranger-general, Jones was now an officer of the crown (the same crown he had taken arms against twenty years earlier).

This new title gave Major Jones many perks—the most significant of which was the monopoly on whaling and other fisheries on Long Island. Jones knew what lay in the waters south of his adopted home: profit. In those days whale oil was an important lubricant and fuel source, and a component of paint, varnish, and soap. The waters off America's east coast were prime hunting grounds. As early as 1670, a writer would comment that "upon the south side of Long Island, in the winter, lie store of whales, which the inhabitants begin with small boat to make a trade, catching to their no small benefit also innumerable multitude of seals which make excellent oyle."

Whaling in the early 1700s was different from the era Herman Melville would immortalize more than a century later in books such as *Moby-Dick,* when whalers from Nantucket, New Bedford, or Sag Harbor (on Long Island's east end) scoured the globe for the mighty creatures. In Thomas Jones's day, whaling was primarily a coastal operation, done—on Long Island at least—by whaling "companies." These, wrote historian Ralph Henry Gabriel:

> . . . were primitive concerns, simple associations of a few men own-
> ing small boats and tools. During the winter season, when the whales
> were in the ocean, these boats, manned by [Indians] and commanded
> by whites, could be seen working their way along the treacherous
> water outside the barrier beaches of the southern Long Island shore.
> When night came these parties would . . . camp for the night.
> Sometimes these adventurous companies would be gone two or
> three weeks down the desolate and uninhabited beach.

"The Great South Beach" is how the early settlers referred to it—a long narrow strip of sugary sand and windswept dunes that extended, in a broken line, along the entire coast of Long Island. Thomas Jones saw there was money to be made here, and in 1705, he received a license to establish a whaling company or "station" on one of the sandy beaches of the South Shore. He was not alone; there were several other whalers working the same part of the beach, which, in his account books, he called Mereck Beach. Five years later—thanks to his commission as ranger—these competitors were either out of business or paying "beach usage" fees to Thomas Jones.

△ *The West End beach still looks like what Thomas Jones might have seen—except for the homes of modern Point Lookout.*

Although it might not seem as dangerous as the long seagoing whale hunts of the nineteenth century, trying to kill a behemoth from a small boat using a spear was still a frightening prospect. Basque whalers in Canada in the early eighteenth century used to recite this prayer before each hunt:

> *. . . Allow us, Mighty Lord, to quickly kill the great fish of sea;*
> *without injuring any one of us when he is bound by the line in his tail or*
>   *his breast;*
> *without tossing the boat's keel skyward, or pulling us with him to the depths*
>   *of the sea . . .*
> *The profit is great, the peril is also great; guard above all our lives.*

Although it is not clear exactly where the Jones company station was located, Ben Sohm of Amityville, Long Island, a bayman whose family has worked the waters around Jones Beach for generations, thinks he knows: "It was wherever the highest dune was," Sohm says. "That would have given them the best vantage point to spot the whales." And, as the beach was a more unstable environment than today, the height and location of the dunes would have changed frequently as a result of wind or tide; meaning in turn that Jones's whaling "station" was probably anything but stationary.

With his landholdings, his whaling business, his appointed official positions, and his extensive ranger-general perks, life must have been good for Thomas Jones. But there were still times when his turbulent past would catch up with him, as another Jones family story reveals. At one point, and for reasons unknown, a warrant for his arrest was issued, and a sheriff's posse was sent out to bring him in. They arrived at the brick house to find Jones waiting for them. He had set up a large table at the entrance. On one side a fine luncheon spread was laid out. On the other side, his pistols. The major offered the sheriff a choice: lunch or a shoot-out. If they insisted on arresting him, he would fight them to the death then and there. If, on the other hand, they would take a message from him and deliver it personally to the governor (a friend of Jones's) they could enjoy a fine lunch together as friends. The sheriff, sensibly enough, chose to eat, after which he fulfilled his part of the bargain, bringing the note back to the governor, who himself then came out to Fort Neck to be entertained and, presumably, to pardon or overlook whatever offense Jones had committed.

Oral tradition, reported by historians through the nineteenth and early twentieth century, insisted that Jones continued to dabble in piracy, smuggling—even slave trading, some have alleged (not so far-fetched: Rhode Island, where he had spent a great deal of time, was a center of that nefarious business in the late seventeenth century). "His vessel was a will-of-the-wisp," wrote Birdsall Jackson, himself a member of an old Long Island family, "eluded all pursuers, and he could sail in or out of Jones Inlet, which was named after him, by day or by night and under all conditions of wind and tide." Jackson acknowledged that he was printing rumors, not facts, but rumors could be a powerful force, especially in the small and superstitious world of colonial Long Island. And of course, no rumor then or now gets the pulse pounding faster than that of buried treasure, which Jones—like any self-respecting pirate captain—was supposed to have plenty of.

The Ghost of Jones

Major Jones died in December 1713 of causes unknown. The man was always full of surprises—and at his death, surely some were surprised to learn that he himself had composed his own epitaph, which can still be read on his restored (and relocated) tombstone today:

From distant lands to this wild waste he came
This seat he chose and here he fixed his name
Long may his sons this peace full spot enjoy
And no ill fate his offspring here annoy.

Seven children survived him—the beginning of a family that would distinguish itself in succeeding generations. Jones descendants became judges and jurists; one went to West Point and fought in the Mexican and Civil Wars; another ran his own fish refinery in Cold Spring Harbor, not far from the freshwater creek where his ancestor had once stopped. But despite the later success of the Jones clan, their patriarch could never escape the shadow of his past, even in death. The old wives' tales started circulating the moment he died. Indeed, his deathbed scene became the fodder for scary, late-night stories that would be told for decades to come. Here's how one nineteenth-century historian described it:

> As Major Jones lay on his death-bed, a great black bird hovered above. As the breath ceased, the bird (which people believed to be a demon) made its exit through the western wall of the house. All efforts to close the hole were unavailing, it being always reopened at night by some mysterious power.

From then on, the Old Brick House, as it was known to succeeding generations, was deemed to be haunted. It actually became somewhat of a tourist attraction, famous enough that the great painter William Sidney Mount, who lived in Stony Brook in neighboring Suffolk County, came to Massapequa to draw a black-and-white sketch of the place. A newspaper account from the 1830s—more than a century after Major Jones's death and shortly before the building was demolished in 1837—described the Old Brick House in awed tones:

This venerable edifice is still standing, though much dilapidated, and is an object of awe to all the people in the neighborhood. The traveler cannot fail to be struck with its reverend and crumbling ruins as his eye first falls upon it from the turnpike; and if he has heard the story, he will experience a chilly sensation, and draw a hard breath while he looks at the circular sash-less window in the gable end. That window has been left open ever since the old man's death. His sons and grandsons used to try all manner of means in their power to close it up. They put in sashes and they boarded it up; and then bricked it up, but all would not do; so soon as night came their work would be destroyed and strange sights would be seen and awful voices heard.

What happened to the house was actually less chilling than what happened to Major Jones himself. Supposedly lured by rumors of treasure buried with the ex-privateer, Jones's grave—placed, at his request, on the end of Fort Neck, close to the water—was vandalized. Some accounts claim that the grave robbers then negotiated with the family for the return of the major's bones. Others, including a *New York Times* reporter writing in 1915, claim that when the family wanted the remains removed (subject as the gravesite was to erosion from the tide), only a skull was found. On the back of the tombstone, almost as if to mock the Jones-penned epitaph on the front, some wag had carved this ditty:

Beneath these stones
Repose the bones
Of Pirate Jones
This briny well
Contains the shell
The rest's in h——

The major's skull became quite an artifact. John H. Jones, the family's otherwise-measured, scrupulous historian, wrote proudly in 1900 of how

△ *Today the remains of Thomas Jones and his wife, Freelove,*
lie peacefully in suburban Massapequa.

△ *The Old Brick House, said to be haunted by Major Jones. Located on the north side of what is now Merrick Road, it became an early tourist attraction on Long Island, before being demolished in 1837.*

"the upper half of the skull was placed in the hands of the writer, nearly one hundred and eighty years after it had been first laid to rest." Presumably the head was reunited with whatever was left of the rest of its owner when Major Jones was reinterred in his current resting place, next to Freelove, who later remarried—to a retired British army officer—and died in 1726. Side by side they now rest, in the back of the Floyd-Jones family cemetery behind Old Grace Church on Merrick Road in Massapequa, about a half mile east of where the Old Brick House is believed to have stood.

Thomas Jones left his mark on early Long Island. By the mid-1700s, maps of Long Island referred to one long stretch of barrier beach southwest of Massapequa as Jones Beach (others called it Jones Island). Long Islanders in the eighteenth and nineteenth century would have certainly recognized his name, although probably not because of the beach, which few had any cause to visit. The stories of Major Thomas Jones's life—and death—would be repeated, however, again and again in newspaper accounts and books, until the 1920s, when the Jones name became synonymous not with an old pirate, but with the new state park that emerged on the beach that had once been a small part of his enterprise and his amazing life.

Apparently, even Robert Moses knew little about Jones and retained the beach's time-honored name for his new state park without much thought. An article in the *Nassau Daily Star* in August 1930 reported on a tour of the new Jones Beach State Park given by Long Island State Park officials to members of the Long Island Chamber of Commerce. One of the visitors asked how the beach received its name. "None could tell him," reported the *Star*. "Mr. Moses was there, yet even he was apparently stumped."

The memory of Pirate Jones, the fables of his treasure and haunted house—not to mention his real accomplishments—had quickly evaporated in the brilliant sunlight of what was already becoming one of the world's most famous public beaches.

CHAPTER 3

AN ISLAND
UNTO ITSELF

"Let us have no illusions about Jones Beach as we found it," asserted Robert Moses, in a speech to the Freeport Historical Society in February 1974. "It was an isolated, swampy, sand bar, inhabited by fisherman and loners, surf casters and assorted oddballs."

There is certainly some truth in those words, spoken forty-five years after the barren site of Major Thomas Jones's primitive whaling operations had been transformed into a dazzling new public beach. The Jones Beach of the eighteenth, nineteenth, and early twentieth century bore little resemblance to the magnificently engineered, painstakingly manicured landscape it would later become. It was rough, raw, often flooded, and constantly changing as sands migrated and storms forced opened new inlets into the fertile bay waters behind it—and then slammed them shut

◁ *Coles Powell, a nineteenth-century bayman who worked the waters off Jones Beach.*

again. Driven by winds blowing off the Atlantic, the dunes on Jones Beach would grow to 50 to 60 feet in height. Ponds of brackish water would develop in the valleys between these dune mountains. On the bay side salt hay grew and spread out like fields of wheat on a watery prairie.

It is also true that Jones Island—as it was once called—or Jones's Beach—as it was once spelled—was isolated. There was no land access, and even if there was, it's doubtful that many people would have packed up their carriages and headed there for a day of relaxation. Through the middle of the nineteenth century, the idea of the beach—any beach—as some sort of giant, outdoor recreational facility was unheard of. The beach was a workplace and a dangerous one, at that. "Early Long Island residents were fearful of the unknown," says Joshua Ruff, curator of the Long Island Museums in Stony Brook. "The beach was a mysterious place, subject to nature's violence. European mythology of sea monsters plus the constant tragedy of shipwrecks kept a larger public from enjoying the shore. Few saw any beauty at the beach."

Indeed, through most of the nineteenth century, a shipwreck or sighting of an alleged sea monster was about the only time Jones Beach ever seemed to register in the public record. When the packet ship *Montezuma,* from Liverpool, ran aground in May 1854, the *New York Times* described the location of the disaster as "Jones's Beach, near the New Inlet, off Freeport, a village in the town of Hempstead, Queens County, Long Island," adding—just in case readers were still confused as to the location of this obscure locale—that it "was not Rockaway Beach."

"Here He Is Again," read the headline of an 1888 newspaper story. "The sea serpent, that deceptive monster, made his appearance of the present season on Sunday last off Jones's Beach." The only slightly tongue-in-cheek story reports the sighting, by two fishermen from Brooklyn, of what appeared to be a snake, 30 yards long. "I took a good look at it, and could distinguish between the glistening dark-brown back and the light gray belly," one was quoted as saying. "The head was even more like that of a snake than the body only it was very big and was held about eight feet above the surface of the water. . . . Once the serpent leveled his head with the rest of his body and blew forth a quantity of foam and water from his nostrils." The article notes that the fisherman had just opened "a bottle of cooling beer" when the monster appeared and quoted one of them as saying that the "shock caused by the sight of the monster made us sick. We did not care to fish anymore and left immediately."

The Birth of the Baymen

As we have seen, the hunting of what must have seemed like real sea monsters—whales—had early on become established as a seasonal business on Jones Beach. As that industry died out by the mid-eighteenth century, new ones developed. The waters around Jones Beach became part of an economic system, geared largely toward feeding the growing metropolis to the west, New York City. Generations of men commuted to Jones Beach to work from the old South Shore towns of Freeport, Merrick, Seaford, Massapequa, Amityville, and Babylon, following a series of creeks and channels and inlets into the East and South Oyster Bays, which lie on the north side of Jones Island. They were known as baymen. They raked for clams and blue-claw crabs, fished for striped bass and fluke, and hunted (which they called "gunning"). These so-called market gunners hunted waterfowl professionally. They shot pintails, red-heads, widgeon, green-winged teal, brant, and black ducks, which proliferated in the bays. Afterward, they would make the trip back to their South Shore towns and sell their catch on the docks. From there the shellfish and birds were put

Looking Southwest from Savage's Hotel   High Hill Beach, L. I.

▲ *This pastoral scene of life at High Hill Beach illustrated a postcard for visitors.*

on wagons or on the Long Island Rail Road and transported west to New York City, so that maybe, that night or the one after, the swells at Delmonico's could enjoy a plate of fresh oysters or a delicious duck dinner, courtesy of the South Shore baymen.

Shellfish and waterfowl weren't the only commodity: The tall, thin water grass known as salt hay was harvested from the bay waters and used for insulation or animal feed. On the beach itself a cottage industry developed: gathering driftwood. By the late nineteenth century, Jones Beach has also become the site of fishing operations using large seign nets. This required teams of fishermen working on the beach, not unlike the whaling "companies" of two centuries earlier. Here's how historian George Weeks described the process:

> The crews would sleep in shacks on Jones Beach and about sunrise
> would launch their dory in the surf, parts of the crew holding the

▲ *This early twentieth-century photograph shows Delancey Powell, who shot ducks and other waterfowl off Jones Beach to bring to market.*

end of the net on shore while the other members would be in the dory, forming a half circle. They would bring the other end of the net to shore and then hauling of the net would proceed with caution and the result would be a catch of a ton of a variety of fish, such as weaks, blues, kingfish, porgies, bass, etc.

Weeks recalled accompanying one of the crews from Seaford around the turn of the twentieth century, when he was fourteen years old. "I would stay on the beach with the fishing crew and look in amazement when the large quantity of fish was brought on the beach," he wrote. Some individual fishermen also braved the trip to the beach. It was common, Weeks noted, to catch fifty or more bluefish weighing twelve to fifteen pounds and many weighing eighteen pounds.

About 1904 a young man arrived in Seaford from the East New York section of Brooklyn. Frank Roach had learned to shoot in the marshes of Jamaica Bay and had come east to seek work on the bay. He became a full-fledged part of the economic system that existed on the South Bay in that era, meaning that Roach, like most of the South Shore baymen, did it all: He was a market gunner, he raked for crabs and clams, he was a guide to the sport gunners and fishermen who came out in winter from New York City, and he was a member of the fishing crews on Jones Beach that went out under such legendary skippers as Ben Rhodes and David Waring.

His grandson, Ben Sohm, now sixty-one, still hunts and fishes on the bay, and recalls hearing his grandfather (who died in 1971) talk about the long days on the exposed barrier beach. "At the end of the day, the nets had to be stored carefully inside boats turned upside down," Sohm says. "The boats would be filled up with sand otherwise." Sometimes, Roach told his grandson, the winds were so fierce that nets would be completely buried by sand.

▲ *Disembarking at Seaford Creek, the gateway to High Hill.*

The life of the baymen who worked the waters around Jones Beach was harsh in more ways than one. In response to a growing sense of concern over the annual duck slaughter on Long Island, market gunning was legislated out of existence after World War I. When the Depression hit, Roach—like most of the baymen—was thrown out of work. Ironically, he ended up on one of the labor gangs that helped build the Jones Beach water tower in 1930, the symbol of the new state park that effectively doomed his old way of life.

The Summer Community of High Hill

Robert Moses was not the first man to sense the possibilities of Jones Beach as a tourist attraction. After the Civil War a new moneyed class rose during what became known as the Gilded Age. These men and their families sought relief from the city in the summer and on weekends, and to accommodate them, luxury hotels and summer cottages began to spring up along the beaches of Long Island, from the Hamptons on the east end to Long Beach on the western edge of today's Nassau County. In March 1881 an extraordinary story appeared in the *Times,* announcing that "a new mammoth hotel" was to be built on Jones Beach. "The advantages of Jones Beach are many and conspicuous," the article states. "Jones Beach is washed on the south side by the ocean and on the north by the broad, breeze-ruffled expanse of South Oyster Bay, so that the land breeze as well as the sea breeze brings with it the salty flavor and fresh ozone which go so far toward the bracing of exhausted and toil-weary systems."

The article describes the proposed, 900-foot-wide, multistory beach-front resort as including a bathing pavilion, a network of boardwalks and promenade, as well as drawing rooms, a billiards parlor, and "all the other accessories of a first-class hotel."

The hotel was never built. A month later, the *Times* reported that the developers were locked in a legal tussle over ownership of the beach with the Towns of Hempstead, Oyster Bay, and several Jones family members. It was not the last time that the provenance of this "isolated sandbar" would come into question.

Yet despite the collapse of the hotel plan, a summer community did develop in Jones Beach—and, despite Moses's selective memory, would remain there until almost a decade after the opening of the state park. In 1897 a member of the Seaman family built a small summer cottage along Zach's Bay, which was then connected to the ocean, on the north side end of Jones Island. A number of small cottages began to pop up along the crescent-shaped rim of the bay over the last few years of the nineteenth century. Before long others were built south across the dunes toward the ocean, across what is now Ocean Parkway. As the line of dunes extending

△ *Several of the cottages along High Hill Beach before they were moved.*
▽ *A postcard view of the Sportsmens Hotel. Note the open-air gathering area.*

△ *A typical summer gathering in High Hill. The little summer colony, located near today's Field Six, was the site of precious memories for its residents. "Golden hours in the sun" were enjoyed by those who spent time there during High Hill's roughly forty years of existence.*

from Zach's Bay to the ocean was particularly high, this part of Jones Island—and the summer colony that developed there—became known as High Hill Beach.

The summer colony that flourished for more than forty years was located about a mile east of where the water tower now stands. This Jones-Beach-before-there-was-a-Jones-Beach had its own docks, its own athletic fields, its own boardwalk—even its own Moses. That would be Moses Hunt, who began sailing beach parties, and later a regular ferry service, out to High Hill—then accessible only by boat—in a ship he named after himself.

According to a 1966 article in the *Long Island Forum,* Moses Hunt the man sold *Moses Hunt* the boat to a Brooklynite named Arthur Horn around 1912. Horn established a regular ferry service to High Hill, on the *Moses Hunt,* from Bellmore. It ran twice a day and took about forty-five minutes.

Whether on a ferry or on a pleasure craft, the voyage was not an easy one. "In a sailboat with a fair wind, the trip to Jones Beach took about an hour," recalled Birdsall Jackson, a Long Island historian and High Hill resident. "If you were not familiar with the many shoals and crooked channels, you might not get there at all." Jackson—whose reminiscences were included in a 1959 history of the Long Island State Parks—also recalled one boater who hit so many sandbars along the way to High Hill Beach that he "he referred to his weekend journeys as his 'walks to the beach.'"

Those who arrived on the ferry, as did reporter Elsa Denham for the *Nassau Review* in July 1928, were greeted with what she called "a veritable surprise." ". . . As we move to anchorage in the pretty little harbor, no glimpse of the ocean may be had. High sand dunes, covered with wild shrubbery, beach flowers and grasses entirely surround the small bay." The ferry docked at a small wharf that thrust way out into the southeast corner of Zach's Bay. Passengers would disembark and follow a boardwalk up to a central pavilion, owned by M. F. Savage. Savage's Pavilion would never be confused with the awe-inspiring structures that would later rise to the west as part of Jones Beach State Park. It was, recalled one-time High Hill resident Bill Wisner years later, "a considerable pile of wood . . . a lumberyard's delight but an architect's nightmare." The pavilion was the heart and social center of High Hill. It was here that kids went to buy ice cream and soda pop. It was here that on weekends, dances and concerts were held. "Here," Wisner wrote, "in an atmosphere redolent with the smell of cocoa butter, for sunburn, and citronella, for gnats and mosquitoes, the adults came to eat or talk or get a closer look at the new people who rented the Smith's cottage that season."

To listen to the recollections of former residents, High Hill was an idyllic sort of place—especially for children. "As youngsters, we came to the beach the day after school closed and didn't go back until the day before it started," recalled Lyman Fussell, in an oral history of his High Hill Beach memories in 1983. "We never left the beach the whole summer. You couldn't get us to go to shore for a haircut or anything."

Most of the families who summered in High Hill lived in Wantagh, Seaford, and Bellmore, although there were residents from Manhattan as well. Monday through Friday, most of the men were on the mainland or in the city working, while the children fished, swam, clammed, and played baseball on a flat section of beach that only appeared at low tide. In a letter, excerpts of which were published in 1999 when she was eighty-one, former High Hill resident Lillian Dede of Largo, Florida, recalled a simple but satisfying existence in the isolated community. "Life was fun," Dede said. "Despite the fact that we pumped our own water, read by oil lamps, and had outhouses."

"Life was simple and good at High Hill," Wisner agreed. "We walked miles along the beach, kicking and pawing through debris and hoping we'd find something of value. We never did, but always we came upon an item of interest. It might be the decaying carcass of a skate or a maybe a dead dogfish, or perhaps some timbers, which our romantic imagination told us came from a ship wrecked at sea. Those were golden hours in the sun."

At its peak, just before World War I, historian Josh Soren says that the colony at High Hill Beach consisted of ninety-eight buildings, including bungalows and summer cottages, as well as more permanent residences, a general store, two hotels (the first of which was built around 1900), and a boardwalk network interconnecting them. "It resembled one of the Fire Island communities of today," Soren says. From 1915 to 1940, he notes, High Hill Beach even had a post office, with its own cancellation stamp.

Although remote, High Hill Beach was hopping, especially during Prohibition. Weekends were notorious for enthusiastic partying. In a 1993 letter, then-eighty-year-old Ann Sheehan of Wantagh recalled sitting on the porch of her family's High Hill Beach summer home as a child, "watching a rum-runner boat and a Coast Guard cutter race inside the ocean sandbar, and seeing men throwing something into the water over the boat's sides." Afterward, Sheehan said, rumors abounded of "High Hill Beach people with baskets, little wagons, and other containers rushing over the sand dunes to collect washed-ashore bottles."

The High Hill Migration

The party ended when Robert Moses arrived. In a November 1926 referendum—part of the long political battle Moses and the state fought in order to gain control of Jones Beach—voters in the Town of Hempstead conveyed lands, including High Hill Beach, to the state. Residents were given until the year 1940 to relocate. "We couldn't do anything about it," Fussell recalled. "They said we could either move the houses or they would be burned down." The residents organized. (They were further incensed at how the boundaries of their lands, which had been in the Town of Oyster Bay—fiercely resistant to the new state park—had been magically rezoned to fall within the pro-Moses Town of Hempstead.)

The High Hill Beach Improvement Association, which up until that time had been more of a social organization, began looking for a place to relocate their summer beach colony. According to Fussell, some of the leaders of the association—including Dr. Elwood Curtis (Anne Sheehan's father)—reached an agreement with the Town of Babylon that would allow the High Hill cottage holders to lease land a few miles east, on what was still Jones Beach Island, just over the Suffolk County line.

In an extraordinary migration, over the winter of 1939–40, about sixty cottages from High Hill Beach were moved about 4 miles east to their new location. The cottages on the ocean were moved by truck. Those along Zach's Bay were put on skids, which were then slid onto barges and floated east down the State Boat Channel. Frank Scarangella, who later owned one of these homes, says he heard that two older women residents "sat at the kitchen table with a bottle of scotch while the house was moved by barge up the channel." He admits that this smacks of legend, but it speaks to the real determination of the High Hill community to survive, to prolong their eternal summer party.

In a sense they succeeded. The houses have all been renovated and expanded, but the High Hill Beach community lives on today as West Gilgo Beach, 5 miles east of the Jones Beach tower. (A few other High Hill homes were relocated within the park, including two houses that were joined to become the residence of the Jones Beach State Park director.) Unlike the scattershot arrangement at High Hill Beach, the houses at West Gilgo Beach are laid out in neat lines, and the community is linked not by boardwalk but by concrete sidewalks. Another difference: There's a small chapel at West Gilgo that is occasionally used for community meetings, but there is no large community hall at West Gilgo Beach. Longtime West Gilgo resident Nate Bard suspects this was because memories of the notoriously raucous parties at the old High Hill Beach pavilion were fresh—and the leaders of the new community did not want to see similar scenes repeated. Still, visiting this gated community of what is now approximately eighty homes, one can get a sense of what High Hill Beach

*△ The 1938 hurricane took a toll on the High Hill area the year before
sixty cottages were moved to make way for the expansion of Jones Beach State Park.*

must have been like. Children play in the narrow streets. Residents stroll
along the sidewalks, greeting each other by name. "This is really small-
town living," Scarangella says. "We know each other, we look after each
other, we rely on each other."

Robert Moses was not charmed by High Hill Beach and, as his 1974
speech suggests, seemed to pretend it never existed. "I suppose he didn't
like the idea of having a community in his park," Soren says. The feeling
was mutual—the residents didn't want a park in their community—but, as
was so often the case, Robert Moses ultimately got his way. Today the High
Hill Beach summer colony is almost completely forgotten. And the High
Hill area north of Ocean Parkway is the state park's maintenance storage
area—a home for old equipment and memories of summers long past.

CHAPTER 4

THE BEACH IS APPARENTLY ENDLESS

Ichthyologists know it as *Hippocampus hudsonius*—a type of flat, bony fish with an odd, horselike head, commonly found along the Atlantic coast.

Thousands of people in the 1930s would come to recognize the sea-horse as the symbol of the new state park on Long Island's South Shore—one of the first of many exquisite little touches that would become part of the Jones Beach signature. There it was, in mosaic tile on the walkway by the East Bathhouse. There it was again, on specially designed direc-tional road signs popping up all over the New York metropolitan area—a reminder that the parkway system Robert Moses and Governor Al Smith had fought so hard to build was complete.

The NO TRESPASSING signs were gone; the private toll roads were gone; the guards and barriers . . . all gone. The way east was now wide open, and all roads led to Jones Beach.

◁ *Whimsical details such as this ship-funnel trash receptacle*
and sailor sign delighted Jones Beach visitors.

△ *"Follow the seahorse to Jones Beach!"*

"Just follow the seahorse to Jones Beach," was the cheerful counsel in an early visitor's guide for the park. The guide devotes a full page to driving directions, which may seem strange, considering that most of those likely to be reading such a guide were already there. It's a reminder that in the 1930s, simply being able to drive to the new state park was almost as big an attraction as the park itself. From Brooklyn and Queens, drivers could take the Southern State Parkway or Sunrise Highway to the Wantagh State Parkway. From Manhattan and Northern Queens, the new Grand Central–Northern State Parkway (the product of another battle between Moses and wealthy landowners on the North Shore) would whisk them into Nassau County, where they could then connect with the Wantagh, which would lead into the Jones Beach Causeway.

Along the way, the specially made signs depicted the seahorse straddling an arrow, pointing the way.

▲ Bunting decorated the new Wantagh Parkway overpass at its opening in 1933.
▽ Construction along the parkway in 1931.

Opening Day, and Then the Crash

There was only about a month left in the summer season when the beach opened in August 1929, and yet 325,000 visitors managed to make their way there. On September 1 alone the Long Island State Park Commission counted 4,384 cars in the fifty acres of parking space. Looking back, some of these late-season visitors must have viewed those golden autumnal days at the new state park as the end—not the beginning—of an era.

On the morning of October 24, barely twelve weeks after Moses, Smith, and Roosevelt had presided over the opening of Jones Beach State Park, a cyclone hit Wall Street. "Brokers were overwhelmed with sell orders the minute the doors of the New York Stock Exchange opened," wrote historian T. H. Watkins. "Everything started dropping." Panic ensued: Several exchanges closed, prominent speculators were reported to have committed suicide, police were called out to manage the crowds that were now gathering along Wall Street. This was Black Thursday, the beginning of the collapse of the great, overheated bull market of the 1920s. By the end of the month, losses totaled fifty billion dollars.

Like a fighter who staggers for a few steps before keeling over from a devastating blow, the full effect of the crash on the economy took some time to manifest itself. But by the spring of 1930, when Jones Beach State Park was preparing for its first full season, layoffs were in full swing. The Federal Council of Churches set aside April 27 as "Unemployment Sunday," food kitchens began to open in the major cities, and in the federal government's first attempt to gauge the national employment picture, it was discovered that three million Americans were out of work (that number would eventually swell to about fifteen million).

It was historian Dixon Wecter's contention that no aspect of American life was more dramatically transformed by what would soon become known as the Great Depression than the use of leisure time. He cited as evidence of this the advent of radio (drama serials were just beginning to appear on the airwaves at the time of the crash), soaring movie attendance, and a surge of interest in home hobbies, backyard games, and participatory sports. Maybe it was because Americans needed to relieve tension, or because it was cheap and available; whatever the reason, parks and playgrounds thrived in the 1930s. Between 1930 and 1940, the number of parks in cities throughout America grew from 900 to about 1,500; their acreage from 300,000 to nearly half a million. "The greatest good for the greatest number was the new keynote of recreation," Wecter wrote.

Clearly, the 1920s vision of Robert Moses and Al Smith to create an accessible, inexpensive beach park for the masses had been what we would call, in twenty-first-century parlance, ahead of the curve. As evidenced by the attendance figure of 1.75 million for the year, 1930 was a good year for the new park and a bad year for almost everything else. And it would continue that way through the Depression. At Jones Beach one could stroll along immaculate walkways and on the new boardwalk, humming the popular new ditty "Happy Days Are Here Again," and not feel embarrassed, especially considering that despite those upbeat lyrics, barely 30 miles away crowds of 2,000 were queuing up for a hot meal on the Bowery every night. In 1930, while the rest of the country began to discern the grim outlines of its economic wreckage, New Yorkers were getting a good look at their grand new beach. And they liked what they saw. In a long feature story that appeared on August 3, 1930—364 days after its opening—C. G. Poore of the *New York Times* proclaimed Jones Beach to be "the most spectacular of all" the many new state parks.

"This strip of snowy sand with its brilliant pavilion not only is dramatic in appearance but was dramatic in its making," wrote Poore, who proceeded to provide one of the most vivid descriptions of the look and ambience of

▲ *This aerial view shows crowds along the oceanfront and bay beaches, with the floating theater waiting for a nighttime performance, July 3, 1938.*

Jones Beach in its earliest years. "The care spent on the color scheme makes the beach scene particularly vivid; pink petunias fill the flower beds huddling close to the building; beach umbrellas festoon pavilion terrace and beach—huge bubbles of orange, green, yellow, red. Added to the fixed spots of colors is the human kaleidoscope, arrayed in rainbow hues, ceaselessly shuttling between the azure ocean and the rose-tinted pavilion."

Poore wandered over to nearby Zach's Bay (which he pronounced "nearly as colorful . . . 3,000 feet of beach, a pavilion, floats, diving boards and slides"). He stopped to inspect the boardwalk, then under construction. ("The walk is maritime in character and has a ship's rail. Ship's lanterns will swing from davits to complete the decorative scene.") He noted the games area, much of which was also in the process of being built. ("[M]iniature golf courses and handball court are among the chief attractions. An archery range with a target made to look like a yeoman's castle will soon be ready. Deck tennis and shuffleboard will be played on the lower portion of the boardwalk.") He even took the measure of the "special beach police." (". . . [M]ostly college boys, smartly uniformed in coats of navy blue and white trousers.")

Poore expressed satisfaction with the cost of a day at the new beach, something that would no doubt have been a concern uppermost in the minds of many New Yorkers in 1930. He liked the fact that there were only two private concessions at the beach (the restaurant at the pavilion and what were called "the bathing accessories"). Everything else was run by the state, which in 1930 seemed almost a relief to beachgoers, who had probably been fleeced once too often by price gougers at private beaches.

Parking fees at Jones Beach were 25 cents on a weekday, 50 cents on Saturdays and Sundays. During the summer season, express buses to Jones Beach ran hourly from four locations in Manhattan as well as from Flushing, Jamaica, and Astoria in Queens. Visitors could also take the Long Island Rail Road from Brooklyn or Manhattan to Wantagh, and then board a bus to Jones Beach.

In an era when people came to the beach dressed in what we would now consider business or even formal attire, and then changed into their swimsuits, lockers were important. In its first full season, Jones Beach had plenty—8,782 to be precise—at a cost of 35 cents per day's rental. The cost to use one of the 809 private dressing rooms was 75 cents; you could rent a bathing suit for 50 cents and a towel for a dime.

△ *In 1936, the East Games area offered shuffleboard and paddle tennis.*

▲ *The Jones Beach shuttle bus transported visitors around the park for free.*

Finally, the *Times* reporter was impressed by the cleanliness of it all. "There is not the usual litter of a beach," Poore wrote. "Not a banana peel or a chewing gum wrapper is allowed to lie on beach or walks. Quiet good behavior is evident."

The Construction Continues

While Poore may have noticed the "quiet," activity on Jones Beach was anything but. In fact, Jones Beach was in a frenzy of construction and expansion in the first few years of its existence. The state park fixtures that would become most familiar to succeeding generations were not even near completion when the park opened in 1929.

The day after Poore's story ran in the *Times,* 75,000 people were in attendance to see Governor Franklin D. Roosevelt back again on a Jones Beach podium.

Moses opened the ceremonies. "We are here to lay the cornerstone for a new bathhouse," he said. "When we brought the governor here last year, it looked very different. But what you see today is only a sample of what it is to be."

"There are 75,000 people here today," Roosevelt said, scanning the crowd. "It is a fine thing and if we had enough bathhouses, we'd have at least 1,000,000 coming to the park. . . . This cornerstone is only a symbol, only stone and mortar. The real cornerstone is the health and happiness of dozens of generations of New Yorkers. That to my mind is the significance of this day."

In his remarks Moses predicted that the new bathhouse would be complete by June 1 of the following year. He was close: On July 2, 1931, the gaudy art deco West Bathhouse was opened. It was dazzling in its appearance and scale—as far removed from the wooden bathhouses then common at ocean resorts as the isolated, swampy beach of Thomas Jones was from the accessible, manicured state park of Robert Moses. It contained an additional 5,400 lockers and featured a large swimming pool, a wading pool, a restaurant, and what were called *tea balconies* overlooking the pool and the new mile-long Marine Boardwalk that connected the two bathhouses.

Designed by the Canadian architect Herbert Magoon (with Moses looking over his shoulder), the West Bathhouse was constructed of expensive Ohio sandstone and brown, reddish, and tan brick in a hybrid style that *New York Times* architecture critic Paul Goldberger later called "neo-collegiate gothic WPA art deco." (In truth, the West Bathhouse was designed and constructed well before the Works Progress Administration was established, amidst the flurry of New Deal legislation passed during the famous "Hundred Days" of 1935, Roosevelt's first year in office.)

△ *Governor Roosevelt at the West Bathhouse Cornerstone Ceremony in August 1930.*
This was FDR's second formal appearance at Jones Beach in as many years.
Two years later, he was elected President of the United States.

These 1931 photographs show the construction of the West Bathhouse and swimming pool.

△ *The West Bathhouse interior, under construction in 1931.*
▷ *The completed West Bathhouse and pool in 1936.*

▲ Alfred E. Smith (striped jacket, without hat) joins the crowd at the dedication of the West Bathhouse in 1931.
▲ This early 1930s boardwalk refreshment stand offered a view from a tower. Note the crowds on what seems to be a cold day.

△ *Film star Al Jolson at the West Bathhouse pool in 1936.*

The twin bathhouses, linked by the mile-long, 40-foot-wide board-walk, were two points on an equilateral triangle. There was one more element to the masterpiece Moses was orchestrating. If the seahorse was the playful mascot of Jones Beach, its water tower became its focal point and true symbol—one of a size proportional to the entire enterprise.

The Tower Rises

When the plans for Jones Beach were being drawn up, the engineers and Albany legislators had a far more pedestrian view of how to store the fresh water needed for park patrons. They envisioned what essentially looked like a giant ball or cylinder held up by four poles: the kind of generic public works department–type water tower that is a common—and ugly—feature of most American communities.

Moses wanted something more, something befitting his grandiose public playground. A lighthouse was discussed. Then a church bell tower. That rang true to Moses. According to an account in Robert Caro's book, Moses whipped out a blank envelope, sketched the tower largely the way it looks today, and handed it back to his chief architect, Harvey Corbett.

Visible for 25 miles and bathed in floodlights at night, the Jones Beach Water Tower was a stunning achievement. Located at the plaza, where the causeway merged with the boulevard, the 200-foot-high tower bade an imposing welcome to generations of families (who would variously refer to the cylindrical tower as the "needle" or "pencil"). In the distance it appeared as a red monolith rising up over the bay, but the tower close up reveals itself to be a far more complex structure. A granite base, sandstone pedestal, brick shaft and copper peak, as well as pilasters, a faux balcony, and narrow, vertical slits gave this industrial-age colossus an almost medieval look. Of course, that was by design—Moses's design.

Moses wanted his tower to resemble the Campanile, the famous brick bell tower that overlooks Piazza San Marco in Venice. But peel away the Jones Beach tower's Venetian shell, and it would reveal a cylindrical, steel tank—19 feet in diameter—capable of holding 315,000 gallons of water. This is the water used to run the sinks and flush the toilets of Jones

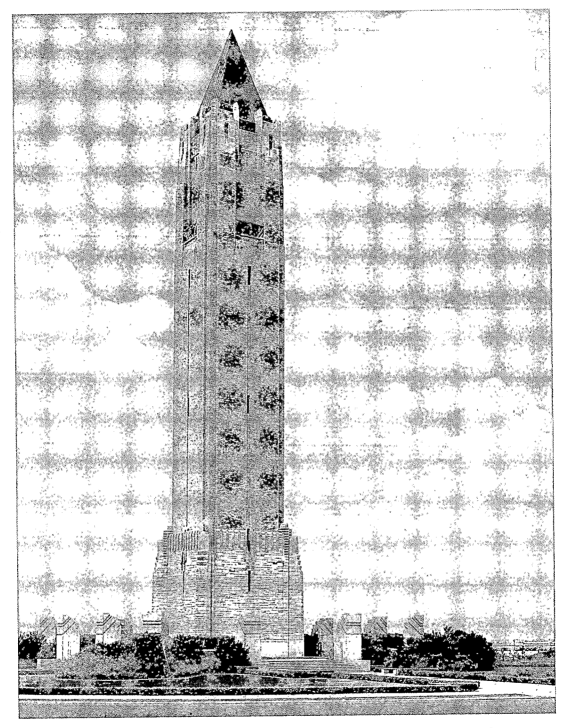

△ *Robert Moses modeled the Jones Beach water tower after the famous Campanile,*
the brick bell tower overlooking the Piazza San Marco in Venice.

Beach. Fresh water is pumped up from three deep wells located within the park, then piped into the water works building, near today's Jones Beach Theatre, where it is treated and purified. From there the water is piped into the tower itself, where it's fed back out to the park as needed (and what's needed on a typical summer day is about 300,000 gallons—virtually the entire contents of the tower).

△ *This 1938 aerial view shows the landmark tower and its symmetrical setting.*

Carved in sandstone on the outside base of the tower is the great seal of New York State, with its eagle, an image of the Atlantic Ocean, and a scroll proclaiming the word "Excelsior" or "Ever Upward."

And ever upward it soars: a 200-foot-high gateway to what even in the dark months of 1930 and 1931 was quickly recognized as one of the greatest achievements in an era of epic projects in New York. In 1930 (the same year the cornerstone for the new West Bathhouse was laid), the Chrysler Building was opened, followed in 1931 by what would become the symbol for Manhattan, the Empire State Building. The new Rockefeller Center would follow in two years. Jones Beach has much in common with these iconic Manhattan structures. In many cases the same people were involved—Al Smith, for one, who as governor had championed the building of Jones Beach and was now the president of the corporation that managed the Empire State Building. More importantly, these buildings represent a shared philosophy of the age—a notion that grand and grandeur could coexist even in the most functional of structures. The Empire State Building wasn't just a giant warren of offices; it was a work of art. Similarly, Jones Beach was far more than just a well-manicured shorefront park. "Jones Beach speaks of a government dedicated to providing a truly noble public environment," wrote *New York Times* architecture critic Paul Goldberger, years later. "This is a beach for the Empire city—not the little beach that you slip away to from a country village, but the monumental beach that you make a long and formal approach to from the great city."

More and more people made that approach. In the depths of the Great Depression, attendance soared. In 1930 there were 1.75 million visitors. In 1931 that number grew to 2.7 million, and then to 3.2 million in 1932. By then the high and the mighty had begun to take notice of "the people's playground."

The World Takes Notice

On October 14, 1931, H. G. Wells arrived in New York. He was not happy. "Wells Arrives in Pessimistic Mood" was the headline in the *New York Times*, announcing the visit of the celebrated English writer and social activist, who is best-remembered today for his science fiction novel, *War of the Worlds*. Wells had come to the United States for a monthlong tour, during which he would issue warnings as dire and Cassandra-like as if hostile, gooey Martians actually had landed in the swamps of New Jersey. Still, given the climate—a depression that was now spreading around the world and the rise of fascism in Europe—his gloom was not unfounded.

On board the ship that brought him to New York, Wells told reporters that civilization was in a state of "probable collapse." He warned listeners of a broadcast he made over the NBC radio network that "If we do not work together, the whole world will bust." And at a dinner at the new Waldorf Astoria Hotel in New York, he warned guests that "This is to be either the hour of human disaster or the dawn of mankind." Not even a visit to the new Empire State Building cheered the dour Wells. "I can't help feel that New York would be a handsomer town if its tall buildings stood on wider bases," he complained.

There seemed to be only one thing that lifted his spirits during his stay in New York. That was an off-season visit to the new Jones Beach State Park. "It is one of the finest beaches in the United States and almost the only one designed with forethought and good taste," he said.

Shortly after, on November 14, Wells sailed home on the ocean liner *Vulcania*. "Wells Goes Home Still Pessimistic" was the headline.

One of the men responsible for Wells's gloominess also had an interest in Jones Beach in the 1930s. In a curious article in the *Nassau Democrat Review* of October 1931, it was reported that Italian premier Benito

Mussolini had appointed a committee to come to the United States and tour Jones Beach State Park, with a view toward establishing a similar park on the shores of the Mediterranean Sea or the Adriatic Ocean. According to the Italian-American real estate dealer in Merrick who was the source for this news (he had reportedly read about it in an Italian newspaper), Mussolini had heard about the park—"greater than anything now in Europe and finer than can be boasted along the Riviera"—from visitors and through newsreels and magazine coverage.

Whatever happened to "Benito Beach" is unclear; still, given the fondness of fascist leaders for enormous public buildings and grand boulevards, it's no surprise that they would appreciate the sheer scale and expanse of Jones Beach, then and now unlike any other beach in the world.

All of this notoriety led to problems. By the mid-1930s, traffic jams on the causeway were common occurrences on summer weekends. Moses had long envisioned a second route to the new state park, this one on the western end of Jones Island in an area known as Short Beach. Getting the state to approve money for his parkways in the boom years of the 1920s had been hard enough. In the midst of the Depression, it was impossible. So a new authority was created—yet another arm of what was in effect the government of Moses, who by then was also about to assume his role as New York City parks commissioner under the newly elected Mayor Fiorello LaGuardia. Moses and the mayor were extraordinarily effective in getting New Deal relief money for New York.

The new Jones Beach Causeway was a typical example and shows once again Moses brokering power, money, and favor to realize his massive projects. The newly created Jones Beach Parkway Authority borrowed $5,050,000 from the Reconstruction Finance Corporation to construct the new parkway (the money was also used to expand the Wantagh

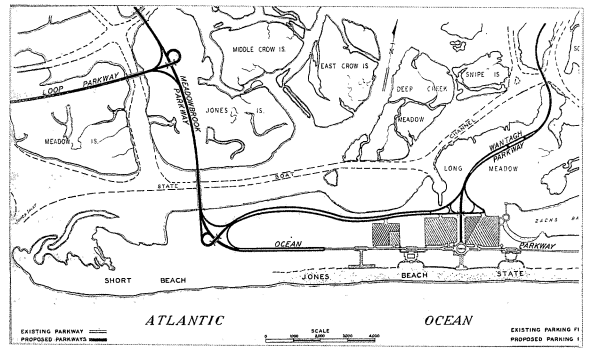

▲ *In this 1933 map, all roads lead to Jones Beach: Meadowbrook State Parkway,
Ocean Parkway, Loop Parkway, and Wantagh State Parkway.*

Parkway and enlarge the Jones Beach parking fields). Once again, the
Town of Hempstead had collaborated with Moses, donating 6,000 acres
of beach, meadowlands, and water rights to build the second causeway. In
turn 4,000 unemployed local men, supplied by the Nassau Work Relief
bureau, were hired to do most of the work.

    The new Meadowbrook Causeway ran from about 5 miles from the
mainland at Freeport across the marshes and tidal meadowlands of Merrick
Bay. About a mile north of the beach, the new Long Island Loop Causeway
split off and went east, connecting with Lido Boulevard and Long Beach.
If the fawning prose of the *Nassau Democrat Review* is any indication, any
lingering suspicions by the locals toward Moses and his state park projects
(or at least any lingering suspicions by Democrats) seem to have vanished
in the wake of the success of Jones Beach State Park: "Opening of Great

▲ *Jones Beach in its ascendancy, 1938.*

Project Saturday Will Fulfill Long-Cherished Idea of Poetic-Minded but Practical Moses," read the headline on October 24, 1934.

An Entrance from the West

There was no doubting the fact that the Meadowbrook Parkway was another "great project." Again, a prodigious amount of fill—this time 38 million cubic yards—was dredged, using pipelines up to 2 miles in length to pump the sand. Six bridges were constructed and—so as not to restrict boat travel—were built 5 feet higher than the ones on the Wantagh Causeway. A total of 1,726 piles up to 95 feet in length were driven into

▲ Heavy traffic along the Wantagh State Parkway in 1932 attests to the early popularity of Jones Beach State Park.

the bay bottom, some weighing as much as thirty tons. In addition to the six channel bridges, three handsome, stone-faced bridges were also erected, one at Merrick Road, one at the intersection of the Meadowbrook and Loop Causeways, and the third at Jones Beach itself.

Much of the work on the new parkway was done over the cold winter of 1933–1934. In addition, the materials and equipment had to be towed in by barge through Jones Inlet—where, according to the old legends, the Pirate Jones and his "will o' the wisp" ship once sailed by night. "The treacherous character of that notorious waterway was a constant source of concern to the engineers and contractors engaged in the work," noted the *Review.*

There had been more of the usual battles offsite as well. In order to pay for the maintenance of the two causeways, a toll was instituted. This didn't sit well with a group of residents in the Town of Oyster Bay, who sued the State Park Commission. The toll charge was upheld in court.

Despite the various obstacles, the entire Meadowbrook Causeway project, including paving of the new parkway and landscaping, and planting of beach grass to prevent erosion, was finished in eighteen months—six months ahead of schedule. By the late 1930s, as the country began to ease out of the Depression, visitors to Jones Beach were pouring down two entrances: one on the east end of the State Park, one on the west. The park was growing—and with it, attendance and attention.

Eleven years after *Times* reporter C. G. Poore took his walk along the still-unfinished boardwalk, past the construction at the games area and bathhouse, Edmond Fish, a writer for the *Saturday Evening Post,* arrived to take the temperature of the oceanfront development that was now renowned worldwide. The *Post* was an enormously popular national magazine, and Fish was escorted on his tour of the beach by Moses himself—who even posed for a photo for the magazine, splashing into the surf, looking quite fit in his bathing suit.

The Jones Beach described in the article provides a neat bookend to the first decade of the new state park that had opened three months before the crash of 1929. When the *Post* story was published in July 1941, Pearl Harbor was just five months away. The country had weathered the Depression. The new state park had done more than survive; it had thrived from the very beginning. Like so many others, Fish seemed enthralled by the beach's unique culture, so far removed from that of nearby Coney

Island, which, the writer described (in language that must have made Moses smile and nod in approval) as "a giant bazaar, an all-summer county fair, a midway of freaks and an orgy of dyspepsia." Jones Beach was different. "Flowers, lawns, shrubs greet you, instead of papers, lunch boxes and dirt. Nothing is crowded, the sidewalks are wide, the buildings are low and attractively designed. The beach is apparently endless."

At the time Fish visited, annual attendance was up to four million a year—still small compared with "the subway beach" (as he referred to Coney Island). Although devotees of Coney, particularly today, sneer at the "sterility" of Jones Beach and wax poetic on the charms of its tawdry amusement parks, Fish appreciated the difference.

"Good taste is the first commandment at Jones Beach," he wrote. " It is somehow impregnated in the atmosphere of the place."

That aesthetic was enforced by a code of rules that included no undressing in cars, no undershirts, and no overly passionate displays.

An army of 1,250 employees made sure that patrons adhered to the rules and kept the place clean. They were distinguished by a rainbow of various-colored uniforms. Fish reported, "There are white-suited parking field men, lifeguards in orange and black, uniformed men and women in the two restaurants and seven cafeterias and snappy-looking laborers in blue dungarees picking up bottles and rubbish."

▷ *A happy crowd found their way along the Central Mall to celebrate Independence Day, 1936.*

*The park's nautical theme extended to its ship-funnel trash cans
and life-preserver-shaped ashtrays set along the boardwalk railings.*

By now people had also noticed the nautical "theme" of Jones Beach, the sense of illusion that transformed trash receptacles into curving funnels like ship's ventilators and drinking fountains into mock binnacles—the cases that held a ship's compass.

And everywhere the symbol of the new reign that had now established and solidified its presence as the best of places, in the worst of times: "From the roadside signs directing you to the beach to the paper around the lump sugar in the restaurant, the Sea Horse catches your eyes," Fish wrote. "He's the coat of arms of Jones Beach."

CHAPTER 5

THE GIRLS (AND BOYS) FROM JONES BEACH

The best thing to come out of the movie *The Girl from Jones Beach* may have been its catchy title song.

All the boys are in a whirl every time they see the girl from Jones Beach
She's the kind of a girl that would fit into anybody's scheme . . .

Six decades after the film's release in 1949, the rest is hard to watch, despite the presence of the stunning Virginia Mayo. She plays Ruth Wilson, a teacher from Meadow Brook Public School who spends her free time at Jones Beach.

Her costar and romantic interest is future President Ronald Reagan.

Reagan, thirty-nine at the time of the film and just starting to get active in politics as president of the Screen Actors Guild, plays the artist

◁ *Celebrities also flocked to Jones Beach. Here Olympic swimmer Eleanor Holm*
elicits a laugh from Robert Moses (right) and Commissioner Osbourne (left).

Bob Randolph, who seeks to use the lovely Wilson as the model for "the Randolph Girl," a pinup girl to adorn ads and calendars. But Ruth wishes to be judged for her intelligence as opposed to her looks—an idea apparently so absurd, at least in the minds of the film's creators, that they have her mother admonish her daughter with such lines as "I don't think a man wants to put his arm around a woman's mind."

To Reagan film fans, one segment of *The Girl from Jones Beach* is particularly memorable. As a ploy by his character to win the affections of the Mayo character by enrolling in an English language class she's teaching for foreigners, Reagan pretends to be a newly arrived immigrant and affects what is supposed to be a Czech accent. As "Robert Venerik," he takes her out for a date to Jones Beach, where they plop onto the sand, with an obviously fake backdrop of the East Bathhouse superimposed behind them. Reagan turns to her and says, "When in Rome, do like they do at Jones Beach," and throws his arms around a protesting Mayo.

Even critics at the time thought it was puerile. "The brand of humor concocted [in the film] is not of a lofty order," sniffed Bosley Crowther of the *New York Times*.

Reading the plot summary, one might wonder: Just where is Jones Beach in all this? The answer: California. Although a few location shots were used, *The Girl from Jones Beach* was shot in Hollywood. Still, the very fact that a movie was made about the beach suggests its resonance in the public imagination as something big, something new and exciting, a place where one might actually meet a woman who looked like Virginia Mayo or a man as charming as Ronald Reagan. Of course, the real girls—and boys—of Jones Beach, the ones who visited the beach on summer weekends in the 1940s, were from a different world than Hollywood. They lived in Manhattan and in crowded, working-class neighborhoods in Queens

△ *The beach was the backdrop for this 1949 film starring Ronald Reagan.*

and Brooklyn, places with names like Bensonhurst, Flatbush, Ozone Park, and Flushing.

The late 1940s would also witness the beginning of a migration eastward from the city Jones Beach was originally designed to serve. Many of the same people who had once viewed the beach as a glimmering destination at the end of a parkway would now buy homes on the other side of the bay from Jones Beach. But before that would happen—before the bright spirit of the "girl from Jones Beach" era—the state park would for several years regress almost to what it had been before Robert Moses came along: isolated, difficult to reach, almost empty.

△ *Children's Circus Day 1938, complete with a staff "Popeye."*

The Beach and the War

During World War II, wartime travel restrictions and gas rationing kept most people far away. On Memorial Day 1942, the *Times* reported that at Jones Beach, "lights will be dimmed, most visitors will start home by sundown. Transportation will be greatly changed, cars will be scarce." Parking fields, the boardwalk, and the games area all closed early. The Boardwalk Café went out of business and, it was sadly noted, "night-time dancing is merely something to remember." In an experiment foreshadowing later trends, the State Park Commission permitted bicycles to be used on the Wantagh and Meadowbrook Causeways. Riders were allowed on the

▲ *Servicemen and their dates danced in the USO Room during World War II.*

right edge of the pavement and charged 10 cents to use the parkways. Still, most people stayed home or went back to visiting subway-accessible beaches like Coney Island or Rockaway.

During the war the Marine Dining Room of the West Bathhouse was converted into a USO clubhouse, accommodating up to 500 servicemen. Those in uniform were also allowed to use the beach's lockers, pools, and games free of charge. These off-duty GIs may have enjoyed a pleasant sunny afternoon at Jones Beach before shipping off, but it was a grim, desolate place for most of the war. With German submarines plying the waters off the East Coast, the Coast Guard and Army troops regularly patrolled the beach.

During the war, military personnel and the public were welcomed at Jones Beach with special band performances and transport busses.

The first postwar summer was marked with a special new flourish: A huge fireworks display—set off from barges anchored offshore—was held at 9:30 P.M. on July 4, 1946. That same evening, the boardwalk, the games area, and the skating rink were opened until midnight, and nighttime dancing returned. Jones Beach was alive again. Its unique attractions beckoned tens of thousands of families, many of them households with returning servicemen and new additions—the first wave of children in what would become known as the baby boom.

Marjorie Weinberg was older than the infant boomers—she was thirteen in 1947, the day she and her family (mom, dad, and younger sister) packed up lunch, an army blanket, and some chairs and headed from their new home in Queens Village to Jones Beach. It was the first time the family had ever visited the famous state park.

On arrival they rented an umbrella and settled down on the sand. "I asked if I could explore the boardwalk," she recalls. Permission granted, she walked just a few steps before stopping. "I could not believe my eyes. Right in front of me were three teepees positioned on a lawn near the boardwalk. The sign read: 'The Jones Beach Indian Village directed by Rosebud Yellow Robe.'"

For the Beachgoers, an Indian Village

Rosebud Yellow Robe was about as far from Queens Village or Bensonhurst as one could get. She was a Lakota Sioux Indian—daughter of Yellow Robe, who was a Lakota chief in 1924, the year he and his people (whose ancestors had been living in the American West for centuries) were finally granted U.S. citizenship. Three years later, while then-President Calvin Coolidge was summering in the Black Hills of South Dakota, the Sioux held a ceremony of appreciation for their citizenship. Rosebud was given

▲ *For youngsters visiting Jones Beach in the 1930s and 1940s, meeting the Lakota Sioux
Princess Rosebud Yellow Rose and learning about Indian culture provided indelible memories.*

the honor of placing a feathered ceremonial war bonnet on the president's
head, a moment that was captured in photos and newsreels. She was invited
to speak at the Museum of Natural History, where Robert Moses was in
the audience. He was impressed with the young Lakota woman. Probably
figuring that anyone who could get the famously dour Coolidge to wear a
headdress must be persuasive, he hired her as a goodwill ambassador.

College educated and a gifted speaker—not to mention an oddity in
a part of the country where few people had ever met a "real" Indian—
Rosebud became what would be called today a spokeswoman for the

△ *Rosebud Yellow Rose explaining Indian crafts to children in 1941.*

Long Island State Park Commission, visiting Long Island schools and community organizations, who, Moses felt, needed to better understand why he and Governor Al Smith had built parkways and new state parks in their neighborhoods. Rosebud went to work at the beach during the first full summer of its existence, in 1930. She started as an archery instructor (because, Weinberg says, it was assumed that "as an Indian she would be familiar with bows and arrows"). It soon became apparent, however, that her repertoire was far greater than helping trembling fingers pull back on a bowstring.

Having researched the history of Native Americans on Long Island, Rosebud began telling stories about Indian life and culture. To children

▲ *This 1933 photograph shows Rosebud demonstrating how to use a
bow and arrow at the park's Indian Village.*

raised on cowboy serials and Wild West stereotypes, much of what she had to say was probably eye-opening. Before long, her informal stories had become a regularly scheduled event and soon developed into a permanent attraction—an "Indian Village" consisting of three teepees and a wooden structure—where she hosted a full slate of free activities, mostly for children. In the summer of 1947, the year Weinberg was first enthralled by Rosebud's stories of Medicine Man and Gray Rabbit, the Village had scheduled events that included crafts and games, songs and stories, and the popular daily turtle races, which always drew crowds of kids and adults watching from the boardwalk. A group of turtles, numbers painted on their shells, would trudge along their pie-shaped segments of the circular racecourse while the crowds went crazy. "We children yelled, jumped up and down, and had fun cheering our favorites on to victory," Weinberg says. "Not until years later did I realize that some of the adults were there to bet on their favorite turtle to win."

Rosebud would direct the Indian Village until 1950. She was one of the most popular and well-known figures on the beach for twenty years and was frequently a guest at the Moses home in Babylon. Her influence on at least one girl from Jones Beach was profound. Weinberg went on to earn a graduate degree in cultural anthropology from New York University. Her thesis was on the Indian Village of Jones Beach; she later wrote a book on Rosebud and her remarkable Sioux family, *The Real Rosebud*. The two remained close friends until the Lakota woman's death in 1992.

Growing Up with the Beach

Harvey Aronson was born in May 1929, just three months before Jones Beach opened, and first visited the beach at age four. At age seventy-five, he reflected back on those days. "I can close my eyes and feel the wool bathing suit and imagine myself making mud pies in the sand and digging holes near the shoreline to make the ocean come up," he wrote. "At Jones Beach, even the ocean seemed different—and the whitecaps brighter and the breakers more majestic."

Aronson described falling under the spell of the beach, including the fantasy-by-design that all visitors were passengers on a great luxury cruise ship. "The boardwalk rails were varnished mahogany, and they were polished daily. My father held me up so that I could turn the pilot's wheels that operated the water fountains, and I waited for the pseudoship's funnels that covered the garbage cans to belch smoke and get us under way."

As a teenager in the postwar years, Aronson would continue to visit the beach, where he posed for a photo flexing what he calls his "barely perceptible" muscles and cooked hot dogs and marshmallows in the picnic fireplaces with his buddies. He would continue to return to Jones Beach as a husband and father. Like Weinberg, Aronson would write about his recollections of Jones Beach. His poignant essay about his life growing up with Jones Beach appeared on the state park's seventy-fifth birthday, in August 2004, near the end of his long and distinguished career as a writer and editor for *Newsday,* the Long Island daily that was first published in 1940.

In 1961 Aronson found himself on a plane with Robert Moses and a group of other reporters. In an anecdote that would also appear in *Newsday* colleague Robert Caro's book on Moses, Aronson recalled the lavish, three-day junket—held to mark the opening of the Robert Moses Power Dam at Niagara—which included a reception where a spouting martini fountain was available to slake the thirst of the guests. At one point Aronson approached Moses, who was in a relaxed and social mood, and asked him which of the many projects and public works projects he considered his greatest. "Without hesitating, he replied 'Jones Beach,'" Aronson said.

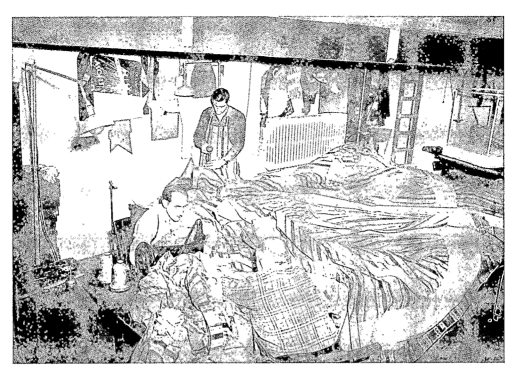

Behind the scenes at Jones Beach: The canvas shop makes and repairs
some of the beach's signature striped umbrellas.

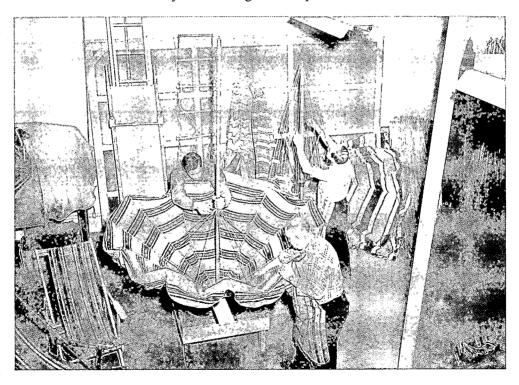

△ *A happy crowd on the beach near the Central Mall area in 1950.*

Moses, of course, always thought big. Thinking back to his days as a boy from Jones Beach, Aronson remembered the little details. One in particular he can still taste today: the Mello Rolls sold at the boardwalk café, cylinders of ice cream that you unwrapped and put in a rectangular cone. They were delicious, just as most of his Jones Beach memories are.

Behind all the fond recollections of Jones Beach in the 1940s was an ambience created and perpetuated by a finely tuned organization. At its head was a fellow named Stanley Polek. In the era of *The Girl from Jones Beach,* he was the superintendent of the state park and the first of several to be identified in the press as "the mayor of Jones Beach." Although a civil engineer by training, Polek—like subsequent superintendents—also

⚓ *Robert Moses speaking at the opening of the state boat channel in 1934.*

had to be a bit of a psychologist and a diplomat to preside over a "city" that could grow to a population of 100,000 on a single day.

"Polek is the head of a little army of 900 men and women who keep Jones Beach the cleanest, most beautiful public seashore resort in the world," reads an admiring 1948 newspaper profile. In the story, Polek (who lived full-time on the state park grounds with his wife Virginia and three children) talked about some little-known incidents on the beach, including the crash of an airliner on the night of January 5, 1947. The American Airlines plane, which carried fourteen passengers, had taken off from LaGuardia en route to Los Angeles, but had become lost in the fog and circled until its fuel ran out. (According to the story, all aboard survived.)

▲ *A baton-twirler was part of the celebration on August 4, 1949, to mark
the twentieth anniversary of Jones Beach State Park.*

Polek also spoke about a ring of car thieves that had been operating at the
beach. They dressed up as mechanics to provide cover for their hot wiring
and lock picking, but were foiled by an alert parking field attendant.

Part of the mayor's job was also to enforce the almost puritanical
behavioral codes that were still in effect in the late 1940s. In the 1948
newspaper story, Polek describes an incident in which those codes were
breached.

> I happened to notice a young man and a girl on the sand one day
> petting a little too enthusiastically. We're rather strict about this
> sort of thing, so I sent one of the attendants to break it up. . . . The

attendant . . . caught the young man's eye; then he beckoned him over and told him he was attracting attention by his conduct . . . and would he please remember where he was? The fellow took offense so I walked over to him. He started to bawl me out, too . . . I said to him: "Your conduct is your own affair. There's nothing personal in this . . . but we have thousands of people here and some of them don't know what's right and what's wrong. Now you do, because you are obviously a gentleman. I can tell by looking at you." He was so pleased to be called a gentlemen, he forgot his anger and smiled. I told him, "We look to gentlemen like you to set a good example for others," and he said he was sorry but he would be more careful in the future.

The mayor of Jones Beach seemed well rewarded for his demanding job: rent-free house, no real estate taxes, free oil heat, the use of a state car, and, "something over $100 a week in salary."

In the newspaper story, Polek sounded pleased to be mayor: "It's a wonderful job," he said. "The most interesting in the country—bar none."

CHAPTER 6

KING OF ALL
BEACHES

Jones Beach stood triumphant as it entered its third full decade. "The King of All Beaches" is how it was described in a 1953 editorial in the *Queens Evening News,* "a spot which other Americans travel thousands of miles just to see."

Royal status didn't come cheap. In a speech delivered on the eve of its twentieth anniversary, Long Island State Park Commission Executive Secretary Chester Blakelock estimated that Jones Beach had cost $15 million in public money and quoted his boss, Robert Moses, as to just why it was so expensive. "We could, of course, have developed a plan which was less ambitious with cheaper buildings and facilities of poor design and flimsy construction. By keeping down the number of employees and not insisting on the highest standards of order and cleanliness, by ignoring the

◀ *Though his long and often controversial career in public service*
helped rewrite the map of New York, many—including Moses himself—
felt that Jones Beach State Park was his crowning achievement.

△ *New York State Gov. Nelson Rockefeller and his wife, Mary, join the crowd
on the thirtieth anniversary of Jones Beach State Park in 1959.*

need of future expansion, we could reduce our charges. We do not wish
to be associated with this kind of enterprise. We do not believe it is what
the metropolitan community wants."

This was the kind of smug language that rankled Moses's critics
throughout his career. But who could disagree with him? By the end of
the 1940s, annual attendance at Jones Beach was nearly five million and
climbing. Over the next twenty years, the number of visitors would
almost triple, to thirteen million in 1968. The growth spurt was linked to
several important social trends that would propel the beach to its peak but
would also lead indirectly to its later problems, some of which persist to
this day.

The Spread of the Suburbs

In 1947, as Jones Beach was enjoying a postwar resurgence, the construction firm Levitt & Sons announced plans for a mass subdivision on the Hempstead Plains south of Hicksville. The homes, which would be built relatively quickly and cheaply and without basements, were designed for returning veterans, 800 of whom showed up at a Town of Hempstead meeting in support of the new development. The lack of basements didn't deter the house-hungry veterans one bit. In an anecdote relayed by county historian Edward Smits, one of the veterans in the meeting shouted out from the crowd, "No cellar beats one room in an attic where you freeze to death!" The board approved the subdivision. By October of that year, the first 200 families, all of them headed by ex-GIs, moved into the new community called Levittown.

Long Island's great postwar suburban boom had begun. The residents of the crowded city that Jones Beach was developed to serve were now moving out to Long Island themselves. Instead of visitors to the beach, they would now be neighbors. In the 1950s Nassau County's population doubled from 672,765 to 1,300,171; the Town of Hempstead (the once-sleepy township of which much of Jones Beach had originally been a part) became the fastest-growing community in the United States as its population almost doubled, from 448,092 to 767,211.

Even without basements, the new Levitt houses offered 720 square feet of first-floor space and included a kitchen, two bedrooms, a bath, a living room, closets, and an attic—lavish amenities for families used to being pent up in the tight living quarters of the city. One thing that most of them did not yet have, however, was air-conditioning.

And so, on the sweltering, humid days and nights of Long Island's summers, many new suburbanites headed south on the Meadowbrook or

△ *With the water tower in the distance, visitors enjoy playing shuffleboard*
at the East Games area in 1964.

Wantagh Parkways to the cool breezes of Jones Beach with their rapidly
growing families in tow.

"It's kind of where I grew up," recalls Greg Karl, who used to visit
the beach in the 1950s with his sister and father on weekday evenings,
weekends, and summer vacations. Karl learned to swim in the West
Bathhouse pool, played shuffleboard and paddle tennis at the East Games
area, and rode the waves in the ocean. Escaping the heat of their North
Bellmore home at nights was a particular thrill. "Going down to the beach
where everything was cool and lit up," he said. "It was exciting."

It was also crowded. Karl was twelve years old in 1957, the year beach attendance reached ten million. He remembers long lines to the diving boards at the pool, the crowded bathhouse decks, and the teeming boardwalk.

Expanding to Short Beach

From his office on the second floor of the bathhouse, Moses could see all of this as well. He knew the beach was becoming increasingly crowded and, from early on in the development of Jones Beach, he knew where the solution to this problem lay. Out there to the west, past the end of the boardwalk, past the Meadowbrook Causeway, was Short Beach—a raw, often-flooded sand spit that Major Thomas Jones and his whaling crews would probably have recognized. At the far west end of Short Beach was Jones Inlet, a treacherous, narrow waterway that, in 1940 alone, had been the site of 237 boat accidents and 840 Coast Guard rescues. Nassau County and the Town of Hempstead were concerned about this area, but Moses saw an opportunity that could benefit all. In 1941 he led a group of state, county, and town officials, as well as representatives of local fishing, boating, and commercial shipping interests, in an appeal to the federal government to dredge the inlet and build a stabilizing jetty in order to reduce the hazards of navigation.

Short Beach had once been bordered on its eastern side by Zach's Inlet, which had closed naturally in 1926, just in time for the development of the state park. Since then, Jones Inlet had been narrowing in width—from 7,800 feet in 1880 to 1,500 feet in 1927. This was the result of sands migrating east to west in a naturally occurring process known as littoral drift.

In a meeting with the board of engineers of the War Department at the Short Beach Coast Guard Station in July 1941, Moses declared the

△ *The West End jetty, constructed by the U.S. Army Corps of Engineers
in late 1957, protects the newly dredged Jones Inlet.*

inlet "the greatest waterway hazard of the whole Long Island shore." The
federal officials then accompanied Moses and local officials on a boat tour
through the inlet and adjacent waters. Afterward, newspaper reports
noted, "They were the guests of Mr. Moses at the Marine Dining Hall (in
the West Bathhouse) at Jones Beach."

The combination of logic, outdoor exercise, and food did its trick.
Three months later, the federal government agreed to the plan. It went on
hold because of the war, but the project was resumed in the 1950s, and by
1957 the mile-long jetty—constructed by the U.S. Army Corps of
Engineers using granite stones shipped from Connecticut—was completed. With the inlet stabilized Moses got to work on developing Short
Beach, which was soon being referred to as the West End of Jones Beach

State Park. As usual, Moses was thinking big. West End I, the first part of the new development, was open in 1960, with a parking field that could accommodate 2,100 cars. West End II, which followed in 1962, could hold 3,200 cars—the largest of any oceanfront parking field in Jones Beach. The addition of the two West End fields brought the total number of parking spaces at the state park to 24,000.

Architectural critics would never gush over the West End bathhouses the way they had over the original two. They were small and designed in modern "municipal parks department" style—utterly lacking in the sophistication and grandeur of the East and West Bathhouses along the main stretch of Jones Beach. Then again, the very concept of a "bathhouse" had become anachronistic. As early as 1948 it was estimated that four out of five visitors to the beach no longer used the bathhouses for dressing. By 1960 a more casually attired population arrived ready to swim. The West End bathhouse, like the one built later at Field Six on the east end of the park, was primarily for comfort stations, showers, first aid, and snack bars.

A *Newsday* headline trumpeted the opening of the additional mile of the West End—including West End II and the new forty-berth boat basin on the other side of the island—as the new "Sun-Fun Mile." Like everything else at Jones Beach, it didn't come cheap: The price tag for winning the West was $1.8 million.

Opening that final piece of the West End expansion on June 26, 1962, brought the length of oceanfront beach to 6½ miles. It also represented the end of an era. "The development of Jones Beach is nearing completion," wrote Moses, who was already turning his attention to other uber-projects: the 1964–1965 World's Fair, for one; Fire Island, for another, where a new oceanfront state park would eventually be developed and, in 1963, named

△ *July 1950: The beach is packed, the West Bathhouse is packed, the parking lot is packed. It was on days like this that Robert Moses looked for relief—and eventually found it in the undeveloped West End.*

after him. (Ironically, Robert Moses State Park would eventually divert considerable attendance from Jones Beach.) Beyond it stood a cluster of bohemian summer communities, much resembling the old one at High Hill Beach. These communities of Fire Island, however, managed to successfully resist Moses. The great builder's dream of one long uninterrupted stretch of state park and boulevard from West End II to Smith Point Park on the east end of Fire Island would never be fulfilled; to this day the Fire Island communities retain their distinct flavor and independence.

In 1962 all that was in the future. Jones Beach was still a brilliant, glittering present to the thousands of visitors who had new spaces to explore. Some were the new residents of suburbia. To the baby boomers—the children of the World War II generation, born between 1946 and 1964— Jones Beach was an exotic playground.

Jones Beach Memories

The sweet smell of flowers or the freckles on a young girl's face in the morning sun, the taste of Mello Rolls or the sound of the echoes in the underpass. Despite the enormity of Jones Beach, it's the little things that people seem to remember.

Roy Peter Clark grew up in Albertson in Queens and attended the elite Catholic high school Chaminade in Mineola. There, he says, "I was a 135-pound weakling who couldn't swim." Jones Beach both frightened and allured him. "I couldn't stay away . . . it was where the cool guys and pretty girls hung out." In June 1966 Clark remembers climbing into his big, white 1959 Mercury Montero with his sixteen-year-old date and heading down to the beach the day after the Chaminade senior prom. Affectionate on the dance floor the previous night, the girl was now aloof. "At the beach she wouldn't even sit on the same blanket with me," he

Pitch putt golf and fishing off the pier were part of the sporting life at Jones Beach.

recalled. Clark concedes that the contrast between him and his young lady friend was probably part of the problem. "She had a nice tan and I was as pasty as a boy could be. I probably looked like a pipe cleaner with glasses."

Clark, who today lives in St. Petersburg, Florida, can still remember how miserable he felt at Jones Beach that long-ago morning. "But I rebounded," he says cheerfully, and without offering further details, "with a girl from Point Lookout!"

Meredith Markfield of Islandia remembers how in the early 1960s her entire block made weekly trips to Field Six, parking together, camping out in the sand together, eating together, all in a sort of suburban communal feast. "The line of cooler-filled trunks became the buffet line for breakfast," Markfield recalled in a 2004 *Newsday* article. "If you didn't like what your parents brought, you just moved down the line. . . . We were a neighborhood in the truest sense."

Jerry Ford's Jones Beach memories are triggered not by the sound of the ocean or the feel of sand beneath his toes, but by the scent of flowers. Ford (no relation to the ex-president) grew up in Douglaston, also in Queens. His family visited Jones Beach as often as possible. "I remember walking from our car to the beach at the Central Mall," recalls Ford, following the trek that was familiar to many: Parking Lot 4, through the Ocean Parkway underpass where children shouted aloud to hear the echo, and then down the paved promenade to the boardwalk. "The flowers that lined the walkway were beautiful, purple, red, and all striped with white," Ford says. "Their smell was like perfume. When I am in a nursery today and smell those flowers, I immediately remember those faraway days." Like many, Ford also remembers the nights at Jones Beach as being very special. The family would walk down to the bandstand, where he and his two brothers would sit eating ice cream and watch his mother and father dance.

"I remember how beautiful and graceful they were," he said. "They just floated as they danced around the band shell."

As the evening grew to a close, the family would walk once more down to the water before leaving. "It was like magic," he said. "The sky, the water. The first time I ever saw the Milky Way was at Jones Beach at night."

Powered largely by the members of the baby boomer generation and their parents, attendance would continue to grow, to a peak of 13.5 million in 1977, before starting a long and steady decline in the 1980s. Jones Beach peaked on its fortieth anniversary. In 1929 the new state park had consisted of one bathhouse linked by a four-lane causeway to the mainland. By 1969 two parkways and a total of twenty-one lanes provided access to a state park consisting of 2,413 acres, sixteen beaches, two pools, two bathhouses, a bay-front theater, three boat basins, six fishing piers, three restaurants, seventeen refreshment stands, and parking space for 30,000 cars.

In short it was a triumph. "Jones Beach has set the standard that other communities all over the world try to reach," the *Long Island Press* editorialized in August 1969. "It's a constant reminder that the public can have the finest facilities possible if it's willing to spend the money needed on them, and if it's lucky enough to have men of vision and imagination around to make a dream come true."

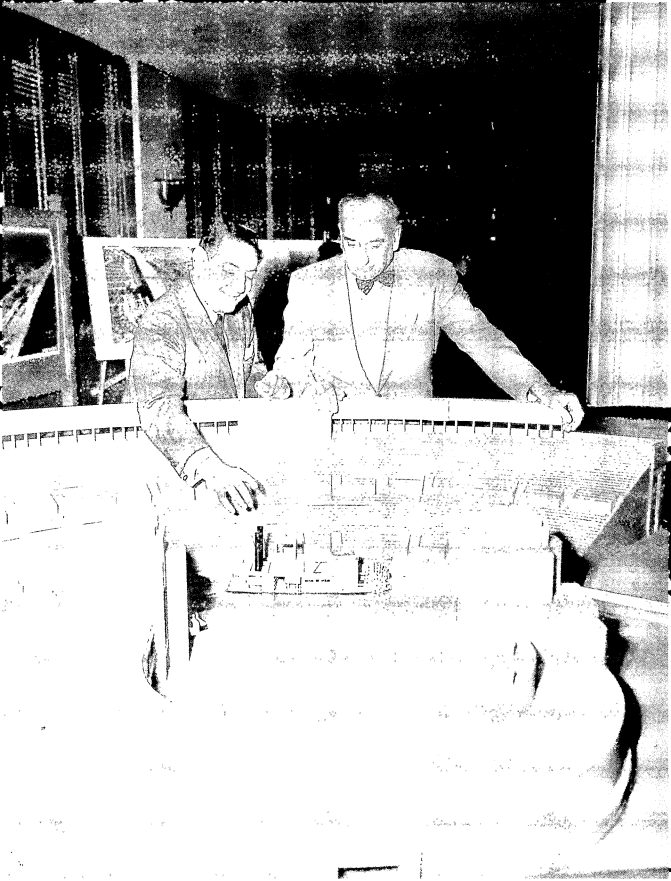

THE GUY
WHO LOVED
THE BEACH

George "Chip" Gorman reported for his first day of work at Jones Beach in May 1977. Gorman was a student at the State University of New York in Farmingdale. In that era, when competition for good summer jobs was fierce among the then-college-aged baby boomers, a job at the beach was considered a plum.

That morning John Norbeck, then an assistant supervisor, later director of operations, sent Gorman off with a work detail to the Jones Beach Theatre. The beach was still renowned for its cleanliness, and the theater was no exception. Gorman and three other young summer hires had to mop and sweep the entire 8,206-seat facility, set on the north side of Zach's Bay. Once the place was immaculate, the young men laid down the black rubber matting on the stairs that led to the wooden seats. This was

◀ *Guy Lombardo and Robert Moses discuss a model for the production of "Showboat" at the Marine Theatre in 1956.*

△ In this undated photograph, Guy Lombardo directs his Royal Canadians while
the crowd dances the night away under the tent at the Marine Theatre.

a precautionary measure; the concrete could get slippery when it rained, a dangerous situation for the senior citizens who made up the bulk of the audience.

Three men entered the empty theater while the summer kids were working. "They were joking and talking together, very jovial," recalls Gorman. "We looked up, said 'Hi,' they said 'Hi.' It's funny, now, that I remember thinking one of them . . . he was wearing an open collar dress shirt and jacket . . . had this great smile."

When the three men passed, one of Gorman's coworkers whispered to him, "Do you know who that was?"

Gorman replied that he had no idea.

"Guy Lombardo," said his coworker.

"And I was like, 'Get out here!'" recalls Gorman.

Everybody knew Guy Lombardo. For twenty-three years, from 1954 to 1977, Lombardo was the executive producer for the Jones Beach Marine Theatre. He did seventeen major shows, from *Arabian Nights* to *Finian's Rainbow*. By all accounts the man who popularized "Auld Lang Syne" as a New Year's Eve standard was a revered and beloved figure at the beach—except, that is, the accounts that considered profit and loss. There, as Lombardo himself would admit, the record was not quite as sunny, despite his disposition and winning smile.

A native of London, Ontario, Lombardo and his brothers—Carman and Lebert—had founded one of the most popular big bands of their day, creating what their devotees called "the sweetest music this side of heaven." Guy Lombardo and his Royal Canadians were a pioneering band on radio, and they played some of the biggest nightclubs and concert halls. Eventually, they became the house band at Manhattan's Roosevelt Grill, where their annual New Year's Eve show (later moved to the Waldorf

Astoria Hotel) was broadcast around the world every New Year's Eve for decades.

Still, as innovative and successful as it may have been earlier, by the mid-1950s Guy Lombardo's sound was beginning to sound out of date—especially to a country about to be electrified by the emergence of an entirely new form of music: rock 'n' roll. Enter Robert Moses, who contacted Lombardo in 1954 to take over direction of his theater, which itself had hit turbulent waters.

Good, Clean Entertainment

The first theater, the Jones Beach Marine Stadium, was a wooden, open-air structure built in 1930. Water shows and circuses—some of them featuring top Olympic swimmers—were held there, as well as the occasional operetta or fireworks display. The original building was razed in 1952 to make way for a grander structure—one more befitting of the now world-famous beach. The new theater had a 104-foot-wide stage, a 76-foot revolving center stage, and an underwater tunnel leading from the shore to the stage. Designed for aquacade water shows, its most distinctive feature was a 100-foot-wide lagoon that separated the audience from the stage. Billy Rose, whose elaborate aquacade shows had dazzled audiences at the 1939 World's Fair, was invited to become the producer at Jones Beach. He rejected Moses's offer, calling the configuration of the stage and the lagoon a "dumb arrangement." Moses then reached out to the Broadway producer Mike Todd, who in 1953 staged *A Night in Venice* at the Jones Beach Theatre. It was a critical and financial flop. (Most notable about the production was the presence of Todd's girlfriend-later-wife Elizabeth Taylor.)

With that failure Moses turned to Lombardo, sending his deputy Sid Shapiro to sign him up as producer. "He said Mr. Moses had asked him to

▲ *Dancers in the 1956 production of "Showboat."*

call us," Lombardo recalled in his 1975 autobiography. "He said [Moses] liked our style, our reputation for presenting good, clean entertainment." Lombardo had his own opinions about Moses. All those years playing Manhattan's Roosevelt Grill had given the bandleader a good vantage point from which to observe and form some opinions on the biggest mover and shaker in New York. "Moses was a hero figure of mine," Lombardo confessed in his autobiography, "because of his penchant for getting things done . . . with flair and imagination."

And Moses got it done. He persuaded Lombardo to take over as producer for the Jones Beach Marine Theatre's 1954 season. It was a high-pressure assignment. By the time the band returned from their previously booked spring tour, they had only six weeks to plan a show. *Arabian*

▲ *Another dramatic scene from "Showboat," accompanied by a full orchestra.*

Nights, a modern musical version of the famous Middle Eastern literary epic, was selected. The elaborate production ran into huge cost overruns. The price tag for the 1954 show was $275,000, most of which the Lombardos had to put up themselves. Still, *Arabian Nights* was well received by critics, who seemed to enjoy the setting as much as the show. "An opulent, sumptuous spectacle," wrote one, "An eye-filling diversion for an evening under the moon and stars . . . cooled by the delightful breezes from the Atlantic."

Moses and Lombardo decided to hold *Arabian Nights* over for a second season. Unfortunately, with many performances canceled because of poor weather, the 1955 production was even more financially draining for the Lombardos. Guy estimated that he and his brothers lost $300,000 of

△ *Democratic Presidential candidate W. Averill Harriman, actor Andy Devine,*
and Robert Moses backstage at "Showboat."

their own money. "I told Bob Moses we were through as producers," he
wrote. "We had loved working with him and his staff, but we just couldn't
afford to risk money anymore on the vagaries of weather in an open-air
theater." Moses would not be denied. As far as he was concerned, there
was only one man to produce the shows at his Jones Beach Theatre, and
that man was Guy. Emissaries of Moses haunted him for the next few
months, determined to get him to sign a contract. Finally, Stan Polek—
the former "mayor of Jones Beach," by then director of operations for the
theater—tracked him down in Las Vegas, where the Royal Canadians were
playing. Polek, pen and contract in hand, followed Lombardo all over
town that weekend. The bandleader finally relented and signed the contract to return to the beach in 1956.

▲ *The elaborate stage set for "Showboat" filled the Marine Theatre in 1956.*

When he did, Lombardo recalled, "Bob Moses had a nice surprise for me." Moses told him that New York State would advance him $250,000 for up-front production money, basically insuring him against losses up to that amount. In effect the Lombardo shows at Jones Beach Marine Theatre became government-subsidized entertainment, one more exam-ple of how, in some sense, Jones Beach was exactly what the *New York Herald Tribune* had once labeled it: "A gigantic adventure in recreational socialism."

For the next two decades, Lombardo and his brothers offered up a wide range of Broadway shows, from *Showboat* to *South Pacific,* some run-ning a single season, some two, and each more elaborate than the one before.

The original Marine Theatre showcased water circuses such as this one in 1935,
featuring elephants, sea dragons, and other fanciful creatures for the
crowds lining the rails and filling the stands.

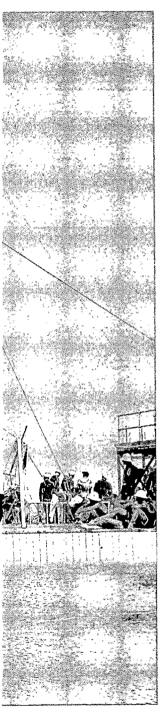

The Marine Theatre floated in Zach's Bay below a popular crescent of beachfront.
In 1939, it hosted an elaborate water ballet for the park's tenth anniversary.

Retirement at the Beach

"I think of Jones Beach as a sort of retirement home for Guy and the Royal Canadians," said the late Chris Doty, a Lombardo historian, in a 2004 interview. "It offered him a port in the stormy music scene of the mid-1950s and onward." If true, it was the kind of retirement home that suited the hardworking but fun-loving Lombardo perfectly. And the commute was great. Lombardo lived north of the beach in Freeport, where he also owned a popular restaurant, the East Point House (he promoted the eatery in the Jones Beach show programs: "The Sweetest Lobsters This Side of Heaven" was the headline on one 1958 ad).

For Lombardo, it was a sweet deal: He was cushioned against further financial loss while producing shows that he enjoyed. He coaxed many of his old musical pals to participate, including trumpeter and New Orleans native Louis Armstrong, who performed at the beach as part of Lombardo's production of *Mardi Gras*. A world-class skipper, Lombardo was also able to indulge his love of boats and joked later about how he managed to incorporate various watercraft in his shows, sailing into the theater's lagoon everything from a Viking ship (for *Song of Norway*) to a

▽ *An up "Tempo" Lombardo on his boat: For the famous bandleader, spending time at Jones Beach was a source of pure enjoyment, if not great financial success. This expert skipper loved commuting to his job at the theater by boat.*

group of speedboats that held an actual race as part of one show's climax (*Hit the Deck*) to an 80-foot barge that was transformed into a floating Alpine mansion for *The Sound of Music*. (A motorboat with a Nazi flag on it was also used in that production, for the scene in which the Trapp family fled the Germans. Lombardo admitted that one day he took that boat out for a ride in the bay, forgetting to remove the swastika flapping from its stern. Boos and catcalls from passing ships caused him to wonder if his popularity had somehow slipped overnight, until he remembered that he had neglected to strike the offensive emblem.)

Elaborate, waterborne productions became the theater's signature. "This is the trademark of all Jones Beach shows," wrote *Newsday* columnist Jack Altshul in 1958. "There are floating vehicles galore because this is a theater on water and Lombardo is a man who loves water and boats."

A Marvelous Showman

Early on, audiences loved the Lombardo productions, held at the "air-conditioned-by-nature" Jones Beach Theatre. On July 19, 1958, a record crowd of 8,588 (382 of whom had to stand) came to see *Song of Norway*. It was another critically acclaimed extravaganza at the beach. "A spectacle to top all spectacles," raved the *New York Mirror*. "A marvel of showmanship."

Which, of course, is exactly what Lombardo was: a marvelous showman. Yet not even his most elaborate productions, not even the addition of such features as the Schaeffer Beer Tent adjoining the theater (under which patrons could dance to the sound of the Royal Canadians for an hour after the show or during rain delays) could stop the march of time and with it, great cultural changes. By the 1960s, people—particularly the young audiences who had once been Lombardo's biggest fans—were dancing to a different beat than the foxtrot or the waltz. Lombardo dismissed rock 'n' roll

Jones Beach Theatre has hosted such memorable shows as "Fiddler on the Roof,"
"Finian's Rainbow," and "Song of Norway."

as "electrically amplified noise" and stuck to his musical script to the end, despite diminishing returns. "I have found something in putting on these shows," he mused in 1975. "It certainly isn't money. There is the satisfaction of seeing all those nuts and bolts fitting into place to provide an audience an evening of entertainment I know they can't see anywhere else."

"They were not profitable events," admits Douglas Flood of the Guy Lombardo Museum in London, Ontario. "But profit is one thing, and exposure is another. The promotion of the Jones Beach facility and showing the world what could be done there helped set the stage for its later success."

Lombardo died, at age seventy-five, in November 1977—a few months after Gorman met him. Although not necessarily a fan of Lombardo's music, the young worker, like most of those at the beach, was fond of Lombardo himself. The celebrity always had a smile and greeting for "the little people"; he was a man who genuinely appeared to be enjoying his life. "I'd see him coming in and out of the theater on his speedboat, the *Tempo*," Gorman recalled. "He always seemed happy, always said hello."

Later on, a memorial plaque to Lombardo would be placed on a large rock, just inside the theater entrance. "I used to jokingly tell people that Guy Lombardo was buried under that rock," Gorman says. "Do you know how many people believed me? But once, somebody broke down and cried when I told them, and I said to myself, 'Uh-oh, this is a bad thing.' I apologized and never said that again."

For the next six years, various producers would host Broadway shows or other acts at the theater with little success. In 1983 rock promoter Ron Delsener took over the lease. "I was a little disappointed when they shifted formats," says Al Keim of Farmingdale, who remembers attending Lombardo shows at the beach with his parents in the 1960s and 1970s. "It was like the end of an era."

▲ *The Guy Lombardo plaque at the present Jones Beach Theatre.*

The New Jones Beach

The new era at the Jones Beach Theatre got off to a bit of a bumpy start, at least as far as Jones Beach officials were concerned. Delsener's first show at the beach, the guitarist Eric Clapton, brought with him a very different audience than the ones that had placidly danced to the Royal Canadians under the Schaeffer Beer Tent. "We were used to older people," recalled John Norbeck, by then the director of operations, in a 1992 *New York Times* story on the theater's resurgence. "Now all of a sudden we had young people. We just assumed they would leave the theater in an orderly fashion." They didn't—security and police were soon beefed up for the concerts, and in 1985 alcohol sales were banned to help curtail rowdy behavior.

Since then, however, the Jones Beach Theatre—now 13,855 seats, the results of two major renovations in the 1990s, including the addition of a second tier—has earned a reputation as being one of the premier concert venues on the East Coast, as magical in its own way as it was during the Lombardo era (and far more profitable).

Gerry Martire, a popular DJ for two New York–area rock 'n' roll radio stations over the past twenty years, grew up in Hicksville and has been a regular visitor to both the beach and the revamped theater ever since. Ear-splitting shows by performers such as Jimmy Page and Robert Plant, The Who, Pete Townshend, Kiss, Aerosmith, and Motley Crue, he says, "certainly weren't what Robert Moses had in mind when the theater was built," but they made it the new hot destination at the beach in the late 1980s and 1990s. "A whole new generation could now hang out in the sun all day, grab a quick shower, and then spend the evening in one of the most glorious settings for outdoor entertainment," he said.

Martire has been there for many of those glorious evenings, but the one most memorable to him was on the hot, muggy night of August 9, 1995. Earlier that day, Jerry Garcia had been found dead of a heart attack at a drug and alcohol treatment facility near San Francisco. Martire had been a big fan of the fifty-three-year-old guitarist and leader of the Grateful Dead. The Allman Brothers Band—another heavyweight classic rock act—was scheduled to play that same night at the Jones Beach Theatre, and it so happened Martire had tickets. At the start of the show, he recalls, "Greg Allman made reference to the loss of Jerry Garcia, and by the time the band was into its long set, a full moon had perfectly bisected the stage and hung like a prop for the rest of the show." The poignant beauty of that night affected the performers as much as the audience. Martire notes that Allman Brothers guitarist Warren Haynes was moved to write a song about the death of Garcia and that night's concert. "The line goes 'We were at Jones Beach when we got the word, saddest sound that

△ *Guy Lombardo (far left), Robert Moses (second from right), and Gov. Nelson Rockefeller (far right) examine a model of the 1961 World's Fair.*

I've ever heard,'" Martire says, "and later the song refers to a 'banjo moon in a tie-dyed sky.' I'll never forget that moon or that night, either."

Denise Rafkind has a favorite memory of a different kind of night at Jones Beach. She remembers seeing the flamboyant funk-rock star Prince play there in 1997. "It was the best entrance I ever saw," recalls Rafkind, who was twenty-five and living in Oceanside at that time. "The lights were on, the music had started, and everyone was standing and clapping looking for Prince to take the stage. All of a sudden you saw balloons going into the air and a boat coming around from behind the theater. It was Prince, making his grand entrance. That was the only time I ever saw a musician get off a boat and take the stage!"

Somewhere that night, Guy Lombardo was smiling.

CHAPTER 8

SAVING
LIVES

Before there were Jones Beach lifeguards, there were Jones Beach life-savers.

Seventy-five years prior to the arrival of Robert Moses, the establishment of a state park, or the sound of the first whistle blown by the first lifeguard at the East Bathhouse, lifesaving stations dotted the barrier beaches of Long Island. The focus of those who manned these primitive structures was a bit different than their swimsuited descendants. They were looking out at the water not for bathers—there were none at Jones Beach in those days—but for ships in distress, of which there were many.

Vessels approaching New York City in the nineteenth century were essentially sailing into a funnel, with Long Island on one side and the New Jersey shore on the other. Storms could drive ships too close to either side

◄ Beginning in 1929, the proud lifeguard corps at Jones Beach
  State Park was led by men such as this captain.

△ *The 1941 Jones Beach lifeguards on the Central Mall.*

of the funnel, where numerous sandbars—located 300 to 800 yards from shore—provided a constant menace. "In a storm, any ship stranded on the sandbars usually went to pieces within a few hours," writes historian Dr. Dennis L. Noble. "Few people could survive a 300-yard swim in 40-degree storm-tossed surf. Even if a few sailors managed somehow to reach the beach in winter, they stood a good chance of perishing from exposure on the largely uninhabited shore."

    To help deal with the growing loss of life and commerce, a network of lifesaving stations was established on Long Island in the mid-1800s. The

△ *The officers of the 1941 Lifeguard Corps.*

first one at Jones Beach was built in 1851 on the east end of the beach. "It really was no more than a boathouse, with a tiny bit of Victorian flair," says John Galluzzo, executive director of the U.S. Life-Saving Service Heritage Association.

In 1871 the U.S. Life-Saving Service was organized by an act of Congress, and the stations became more permanent structures. There were thirty-two on Long Island, spaced roughly 5 miles apart, from Montauk on the island's eastern tip to Sheepshead Bay in Brooklyn. Three of these were on Jones Beach: the original one on the east end (sometimes referred

Guarding lives at Jones Beach, 1939: Early on, the Jones Beach lifeguards acquired a reputation for being the best in their business.

▲ *Jones Beach lifeguards at a competition in Ocean City, New Jersey, in 1934.*

△ *A postcard view of the High Hill Life-Saving Station.*

to as Jones Beach East), another at Zach's Inlet (on Hill High, near where the High Hill Beach colony would later form), and a third on the section known as Short Beach (now the West End of Jones Beach State Park).

One local historian described the stations at Jones Beach as looking like modified Cape Cod cottages, painted white. Each station had a pair of huge doors on the side fronting the ocean, through which the lifeboat could be hauled. There was also a glass-encased cupola on the roof for observation. During the peak shipwreck season, from November to April, the stations would be constantly manned by a captain (called a *keeper*) and six to eight surfmen, who were paid about $60 a month. The crews earned their pay, and not just when there was an emergency. The Life-Saving Service mandated rigorous, daily training for the crews, and given the complexity of the rescue systems involved, as well as the physical demands, such preparations were a necessity.

Springing to Action

When a ship in distress was spotted—either by patrols on the beach or signals sent by the ship—they sprang into action. Six of the surfmen would launch the sturdy, 36-foot-long lifeboat and—along with the keeper—row to the stricken vessel, while the rest of the men would remain on shore to assist. In wrecks close to shore, or if the sea was too rough to launch the boat, the surfmen would fire a thin messenger line from a cannonlike beach gun, hurling the line out as far as 600 yards into the water. A cartful of apparatus, including a tally board (with written instructions on what to do) would be attached to the line and pulled in by the ship's crew at the other end. A heavy line called a hawser and an additional medium-weight line, the whip, were then tied to the messenger line by the lifesavers on shore and pulled to the wreck by the endangered sailors. The hawser was used to support a traveling block, a two-wheeled mechanism that ran along the top on the line, and a life ring sewn into a heavy pair of canvas breeches was hung on the whip.

Once this intricate rope-and-pulley system was in place, Galluzzo says, "it formed a complete circle, like a moving clothesline, and allowed the lifesavers to pull the victims of a shipwreck, one at a time, to safety."

This was demanding, dangerous work, often conducted in terrible weather. And even during downtime, when there were no ships in distress nearby and the day's training was done, the life of the lifesaver—particularly the lifesaver on remote Jones Beach—was a lonely and harsh one.

What kind of men would do this work?

In 1877 a *New York Times* reporter traveled to U.S. Life-Saving Service stations from Block Island to Brooklyn to report on the lives and adventures of the surfmen. Many of those he encountered were fishermen and sailors who had traveled all over the world. "All of them, nearly, have risked their lives in the sea over and over again to save their fellows," wrote the journalist, who described the lifesavers he met as "a hardy, manly, brave class of men . . . with broad shoulders and strong muscles, and their faces hidden behind great black beards. Most of them are tall and strong, and many of them are almost giants."

They were also daring, as evidenced by the rescue of a shipwreck on Jones Beach in 1895. On the night of January 14, a coal barge, the *Seth Low*, with a crew of five, ran aground during a storm. A beach patrol from the Short Beach station spotted their distress signals at about 1:00 A.M., and before long the crews of all three Jones Beach lifesaving stations were on the scene. Because of the heavy seas, the surfmen at first tried shooting rescue lines out to the ship. This was unsuccessful. At dawn the first of many attempts was made to launch a boat to reach the stricken vessel. But huge waves drove the surfmen back each time. Finally, it was determined that the *Seth Low* had sunk, presumably with all hands. But in the afternoon the keeper of the Zach's Inlet station—Philip Chichester—decided to make one last rescue effort by boat. A newspaper story recounted what happened then:

> After several attempts, their surfboat was run safely through the breakers. The wreck was reached, after a hard struggle, without mishap. The life-saving crew was startled to find three men, alive, lashed to the cabin roof. After a little careful manipulation, the shipwrecked men were taken off the wreck. The return journey was more difficult than the outward trip. The crew found it impossible to get back to their own station and was forced to row to the station on Oak Island, about 12 miles east of Zach's Inlet. There they succeeded in making a safe landing.

▲ *Winners of the 1933 National Lifeguard Championship, the Jones Beach*
team poses on the Central Mall with its trophies.

"They Looked Like Gods to Me"

In 1915—after forty-four years of service—the U.S. Life-Saving Association became part of the Coast Guard. Fourteen years later, ads in local newspapers advertised for a new breed of surfmen—individuals who would brave their lives in the same ocean waters, but in a beach environment far different than the desolate, empty waste that the lifesavers once patrolled. They would become the Jones Beach lifeguards.

△ *"The closest thing to military camp you could imagine."*

The men who reported to work under their first captain, William John, in August 1929 were not the hirsute, beefy fishermen and sailors who had inhabited the old Life-Saving Stations. This was a young crew, mostly high school and college swimmers from Nassau and Queens, supervised by a few older men, some of whom had probably worked at other area beaches. In structure and temperament the early Jones Beach lifeguard corps sounds every bit as disciplined as their nineteenth- and

early-twentieth-century counterparts. There was a hierarchy: captain, lieutenant, boatswain, lifeguards. Everyone was clean shaven; appearance was
important. Guards were ordered to get somewhere in "double time."

"It was the closest thing to military camp you could imagine,"
recalled Reggie Jones, who started at the beach in 1944 and recalled his
early days in a 1998 interview. "We lined up like soldiers at the Central
Mall, at stiff attention, and we had to stand inspection. I was a young kid,
facing the Atlantic, scared to death!"

Jones, a wrestling star at Baldwin High School, had been lured to the
beach by meeting some of the young guards who would stop by his
father's filling station in Baldwin. "They looked like gods to me," Jones
recalled.

George Marth was simply searching for gainful summer employment
when he took the lifeguard test. "I was looking for a good job, and I knew
this was a good job," said Marth, a 6-foot, 210-pound high school football
player from Queens Village. He started at the beach on July 4, 1946. "It was
a hot, hot day," Marth, now seventy-six, recalls. "I reported to the East
Bathhouse, and a lieutenant said, 'OK, take this rookie down to the beach
and open up the stand.'" When Marth and his senior partner climbed up
the stand, the younger guard looked around and was flabbergasted. "I
thought I was at home plate at Yankee Stadium," he recalled. "There must
have been 100,000 people there."

Barely ten minutes on the job, Marth was involved in his first rescue.
"All of a sudden the guard I was with jumped off the stand and went running out into the water," recalls Marth, who immediately followed. "He
had spotted a big guy, flailing away in the water. He couldn't swim a stroke
and had got sucked out over his head." During the rescue, the panicked
victim—Marth estimates he must have been stood about 6 feet, 4 inches

and weighed 230 pounds—almost "took off our heads" as he tried to grab hold of something. After he was safely brought ashore, Marth recalls, "I thought, 'Boy, this is going to be a tough job.'"

It was, for a number of reasons: The corps was smaller, the crowds were larger, and the ocean was different, potentially more dangerous than it is today. Because the stabilizing jetty had not yet been built on Jones Inlet, the seabed was irregular, and the same sandbars that had grounded sailing ships in the nineteenth century helped create an irregular bottom. This, in turn, caused a tremendous undertow—the phenomenon that occurs when water carried by waves onto a beach escapes rapidly back to sea, forming an almost suctionlike effect that can knock a person off his or her feet.

According to a 1948 Long Island State Park report, the Jones Beach lifeguard patrol system consisted of a captain, seven lieutenants, seven boatswains, and eighty guards. Each

⚠ *Standing tall on the Central Mall: The 1934 North Atlantic Lifeguard Champions.*

lieutenant had charge of 1,000 feet of beach with one boatswain and twelve guards divided into two shifts: 8:00 A.M. to 5:00 P.M. and 11:00 A.M. to 8:00 P.M. For every 175 feet of beach, an 8-foot-high lookout stand with two guards was posted. Although surfboards and boats were available, most rescues were made by guards on shore using balsawood torpedo buoys and ¼-inch line attached to a reel. The procedure involved one guard swimming out while carrying the buoy, which he used as a flotation device to help support the victim and await the assistance of another guard. In case of a riptide that was pulling the guard and the victim away from the beach, the line was used to pull both in from shore.

The guards were doing their job well. According to the report, there were 1,709 rescues in 1947 and no drownings. But compared with today, there was little formalized training. On the job is how Jay Lieberfarb, then a student at Adelphi University, learned during his first summer at Jones Beach in 1956. And one of his most important lessons was that the life of the lifeguard at Jones Beach was about as predictable as the weather. The first month was quiet. "Everybody said, 'Just wait until July fourth,'" he recalls. "Then July fourth came and went, it was a calm day, no problems." The following Sunday, the beach was, in Lieberfarb's words, "mobbed." Traffic had backed up to Merrick Road on both the Wantagh and Meadowbrook Parkways—not uncommon in the 1950s—and this time, unlike the Fourth of July, the sea was turbulent, or in the parlance of the guards of that era, "like a washing machine."

Lieberfarb estimates he was on the stand for about a minute, when "Suddenly we hear a whistle blowing from the main stand," he said. "They're pointing. Then they're screaming. I said, 'What are they talking about?' We stood up but the waves were so big, we couldn't see beyond them." Suddenly, through the roar of the surf, he heard screaming. There

▲ *Lifeguards man the stands even on cold and stormy days.*

was a woman out there, being battered by the waves. "I could hardly make her out because her white bathing cap blended in with the white foam of the water," he recalled. "I said, 'Oh my God.'"

Lieberfarb grabbed the buoy, jumped off the stand, and ran into the water. There was one problem. "I had never entered the ocean with waves," said Lieberfarb, a native of Queens. "I had grown up swimming in Rockaway and Coney Island, where they had little waves. Nothing like this!"

Plunging into a heavy sea carrying a ten-pound, buoyant object across your chest is a tricky business—the waves can grab it, and you, and send you right back to shore. "Nobody had ever taught me this," Lieberfarb said, "so I go running helter-skelter into a wave and the next thing I know, I'm sitting on my ass on the beach. A thousand people are standing there and staring at me, I knew this woman was dying, and I'm just sitting there." Lieberfarb got up and charged into the water again. Same result. At that point, a veteran guard from the main stand dived in and rescued the woman. "I go back to the stand, and my lieutenant, the toughest guy I ever worked with—he had been a marine at Okinawa—started screaming and cursing at me, with all these hundreds of people looking on," he said. "I thought to myself, 'That's it. My short and happy career as a lifeguard is over.'"

But it wasn't. After the angry lieutenant stormed off, Lieberfarb climbed back onto his stand and within moments was called out on another rescue, which this time he was able to make. Then another, and another. "By the end of the day, I had made a bunch of rescues. I don't remember the details of any of them, except for the first one that I didn't make. But that's how you learned."

Changing Times

The Jones Beach lifeguards could buck the waves, but not the tides of time. The rigid sense of militarylike discipline—imposed from the top by Moses and enforced in part by guards who were themselves veterans of World War II and Korea—began to wear thin during the sixties. In 1965 the lifeguards formed a union and agreed to let New York labor leader Larry Byrne, president of Local 361 of the Building Services Employee International Union, represent them. Byrne negotiated with Sid Shapiro, by then the head of the Long Island State Park Commission, and after hard bargaining, won a few concessions, particularly on the commission's tendency to send lifeguards home, without a full day's pay, when the weather was inclement. In 1968 the state set a new age limit, thirty-five, for lifeguards. The union held a meeting at a motel on Sunrise Highway, where Reggie Jones, already older than forty, delivered an emotional speech, trying to establish solidarity between the concerns of the young and old lifeguards. The so-called "Cloud over Kansas" speech was recounted by former lifeguard and writer Greg Donaldson years later: "My wife told me that I shouldn't stick my neck out for you young kids. But I complained to the state when they sent new guys home on rainy days. Hell, they'd send you home with no pay when there was a cloud over Kansas. I stood up for you and now they want to fire me because I'm over thirty-five."

The lifeguards voted to strike. A week later, the age ceiling was revoked. "They never thought a bunch of lifeguards would get together and strike on them," recalled Jones.

The legacy of that labor tumult in the late 1960s is the continued presence of older guards. It's doubtful that anyone listening to Jones's "Cloud over Kansas" speech would have imagined that the already-senior man of 1968 would still be on duty in 2006. But he is. As are many other thirty-, forty-, and fifty-year veterans—all of whom, it should be noted, still have to pass the same rehire test that all returning lifeguards take at the beginning of the season, which involves swimming 100 yards in less than one minute, twenty seconds and running a quarter mile in two minutes, five seconds.

On Memorial Day weekend 1971 the lifeguards went out again—this time when management announced an across-the-board 25 percent pay cut. They set up picket lines on Merrick Road and Sunrise Highway. "The Teamsters wouldn't cross," said Lieberfarb, one of the strike leaders. "In three days, the state ran out of supplies at Jones Beach and Robert Moses State Park."

▲ *Jay Lieberfarb (bottom, far right) and the Field Six lifeguard team in 1973.*

The state tried to keep the beaches open, however, hiring Pinkerton guards to supplement the Parks Police, who patrolled the ocean and bay, often restricting bathers to knee-deep water. To help break the strike, 150 nonunion lifeguards were hired. Few of them, however, had any training. Two senior lifeguard officials who had been asked to put them through a crash training course refused and were fired. Meanwhile, as beaches were periodically closed because of insufficient supervision, the state was losing an estimated $130,000 a day. Worse, by midsummer, there had been a total of four drownings on Jones Beach and Robert Moses State Parks. The fourth fatality was nineteen-year-old Roberto Colon of Manhattan, who, according to a newspaper account, was pulled out of his brother's grip by a severe undertow at Jones Beach and carried out to sea.

The next day, July 27, the union and the state reached a settlement. Striking lifeguards were rehired, and instead of a pay cut the guards got a 12½-cent-per-hour raise, to $3.35 per hour.

Around the same time the lifeguards were getting unionized, another major change in the lifeguard labor force was made, with the addition of women guards. Marth was water safety director—a position created in the 1960s that involved supervision of the entire Lifeguard Corps—when that new policy went into effect in June 1968. "It wasn't a big deal," Marth said. "I knew that some of the women were very good swimmers. Some of them could beat a lot of the guys." Jones says he heard some grumbling among the ranks, but claims to have responded in inimitable fashion: "I said, 'Wait a minute guys, you been chasing women all your life and now you're going to get a chance to sit on the stand with them! What's wrong with you?' "

Currently, thirty-eight of the 252 Jones Beach lifeguards are women.

Along with the demographics, the nature of the job itself has changed as well. Years ago, "spectacular" rescues involving multiple guards, boats, and sometimes even helicopters were not uncommon. Such a rescue was described in detail in the debut issue of the Jones Beach Lifeguard Corps newsletter, *The Bucket and Buoy*, on July 22, 1975.

Police and lifeguards that week had responded to a call from the friend of a man who had been swept off the West End jetty. Lifeguard Jim Zellner arrived and spotted the victim approximately ¾ of a mile out. According to the newsletter item:

> Zellner made his way out with water constantly breaking over the
> jetty and him. The man was too weak to walk and Zellner tried to
> assist him several feet at a time as the waves permitted. After a few

more steps, Zellner was swept off the jetty by himself and made his way back only because the buoy had lodged in the rocks and he was tethered to it. He was now ten yards away from the victim and had to crawl back to him. Field and two other lifeguards tried to get out a line to Zellner. Field was swept off the jetty and had to be pulled back.

Eventually a Coast Guard boat got close enough to rescue both the victim and the lifeguards—all four of whom were injured in the heroic and dramatic rescue attempt.

Such scenes, although no doubt thrilling to see, are happily not common at Jones Beach today, where the prevailing philosophy is what Water Safety Director Joe Scalise calls "preventive maintenance" lifeguarding. This involves taking more precautionary measures—such as limiting the distance bathers can go out into the water (no more than 25 yards offshore) and spotting potential problems before they happen. "The best rescue," Scalise says, "is to go out to someone not in trouble yet, but possibly on his way, and say 'It's time to come in now.'"

The strategy has apparently worked: As of this writing, the last drowning on a supervised beach within Jones Beach State Park was in 1997 at Zach's Bay.

Perhaps it is this proficiency that helps give the Jones Beach lifeguards a mystique, as well as a bond, as powerful as the ocean they have seemingly mastered.

"It wasn't a job, it was a calling," recalled Greg Donaldson, who chronicled his twenty-year career as a Jones Beach lifeguard in *New York* magazine in 2000.

"It may sound like a bit of a cliché, but it really is a family," agrees eleven-year lifeguard Corinne Peters, whose sixty-year-old, superfit father Ed is still on the job, after forty-three years, at West End II.

"We do have an unshakable bond between us," says Bernadette Mearini, a six-year vet who, like most of those on Jones Beach beach, worked her way up the lifeguard hierarchy, starting from when she was a sixteen-year-old lifeguard at her community pool in Valley Stream.

For her, working as a lifeguard on the King of All Beaches represents the pinnacle of the profession. "We train hard together," she says, "we work closely and rely on each other to do a very serious job."

CHAPTER 9

A SPORTING LIFE, AN ENDLESS SUMMER

At Jones Beach 271,000 people have turned their back to the ocean . . . again.

It's a year later, 2006, and the crowd for the air show has almost doubled in size. It's the largest single-day attendance of any Memorial Day weekend in Jones Beach history, and this time they're here to see the Navy's Blue Angels performing. Their blue-and-yellow, twin-engine F-18s are even flashier and louder than the Air Force Thunderbirds that highlighted the show the previous year.

When, as part of their performance, one of the jets comes screaming overhead from the north at low altitude, blasting out to sea, a man by the Central Mall cries, "It looked like he was going to hit the tower!" Hardly, but the Angels' precision flying around the tower, over the bathhouse

◄ *How sweet it is: Sculpting the cake for the fiftieth anniversary celebration of Jones Beach State Park, 1969.*

spires, along the ocean, and high into the blue spring skies draws gasps, cheers, and pumped fists from the crowds—only 40 percent of whom arrive in bathing suits despite the warm temperatures on this day, and about 100 percent of whom seem to have brought along a camera or digital recorder.

These people could care less about sand and sea. They have come for air.

The record crowds are cause for both celebration and concern among beach management. In one sense it was 1950 all over again: Traffic was backed up from the beach to Merrick Road on both the Wantagh and Meadowbrook Parkways, something almost unheard of in the past three decades. However, by 2:00 P.M., Fields 1 through 6 were filled to capacity. The State Park Police were driving along the parkways announcing that there was no parking, and people would have to either turn around or pull over on the side of the road to watch the show.

No parking! Robert Moses would be spinning in his grave. Especially because the very area that he had developed to accommodate crowds like this, the West End, was closed. "I've got 3,000 parking spaces out there I can't use," sighed New York State Parks Commissioner Bernadette Castro.

West End Story

The reasons why the empty big, empty lots at West End I and II can't be made available for drivers at the time they are needed most are complex and speak to the changes at Jones Beach over the past thirty years. Beach attendance reached a peak in the 1970s, then began a long and precipitous decline the following decade. What caused the drop is a question oft debated by the parks people. In truth there are probably many factors: Most homes now have air-conditioning, and residents don't need to escape to the beach for relief. More Long Islanders have backyard pools. Many stores are

The 1940s saw increasing activity at the park, from skating to swimming.

▲ *Baseball was a big draw at Jones Beach, with fields near the East Bathhouse.*

now open on Saturdays and Sundays, malls are air-conditioned, and people work on weekends. Throw in the Internet, DVDs, cable TV, and all the technological diversions of the modern world, and a relaxing, daylong trip to the beach seems, in some ways, as quaint as a carriage ride in the country.

At the West End of Jones Beach, the problem of declining attendance was exacerbated by the size of the beach itself. The jetty that had helped raise the low-lying natural beach by capturing sand migrating west along the coast did its job too well. The sand continued to pile on over the years so that the distance from the West End II parking lot to the water's edge is now about 500 yards—nearly twice as far as any other section of beach in the park and a long enough walk to deter many beachgoers, who sim-

⚠ *Women's leagues, such as this one in 1940, also played at the beach in front of packed crowds.*

ply abandoned the West End for the easier-access beaches further east.

In 1991 state budget cuts forced the closure of West End I and lim-
ited use of West End II to weekends. At that time it was estimated that out
of the total beach attendance, only a small fraction—about 175,000—used
this part of the beach. What happened over the next decade is that nature
began to reclaim the area once known as Short Beach. Dune grass grew;
plants and animal life flourished.

In 1998, New York State Governor George Pataki was on a helicop-
ter tour of Jones Beach with Parks Commissioner Castro, when he pointed
out the old West End I concession building and the empty parking lot adjacent to it. "What's that?" he asked. When told, he responded that certainly

△ *The fun continued into the 1950s, with paddle tennis and shuffleboard courts, and the teepees of Indian Village beyond.*

a building with all that parking in such a pristine part of the beach could be used for something. Like? "A nature center!" Pataki said, in a flash of inspiration. So it was that in 2000, the new Theodore Roosevelt Nature Center—named after Long Island native and ardent outdoorsman Theodore Roosevelt—was opened at West End I. It now attracts thousands of schoolchildren and visitors every year, who learn about the ecology of the beach, the ocean, and sea life. Environmental regulations carefully restrict what else can be done at the West End. So although it has become a haven to beachcombers, surfers, and surfcasters, and of course to the piping plover, the thousands of parking spaces originally designed to handle just the kind of overflow that beach management is dealing with during the air show cannot be used—even for one day.

It's moments like these, Castro admits, when she almost envies the power of her legendary predecessor. "Robert Moses could have built a pyramid if he wanted on Jones Beach and nobody would have said anything," she says, with

▲ *The East Games area in 1935 hosted bocce, croquet, and paddle tennis.*

a laugh. "He had the funds . . . he *controlled* the funds. Besides, there were no wetlands laws, none of the protections we have in place today for the environment or for historic preservation."

She is quick to add that she fully supports those protections—assaults on which are still regularly repelled. For example, in recent years entrepreneurs have approached the state about building all kinds of permanent "attractions" on the beach, from aquariums to paragliding schools. With the exception of the nature center, all have been rejected. Instead, efforts to restore the beach structure to something close to the original 1930s look have been undertaken, with some success. Today annual attendance at the beach is steady at about five million. A hot, sunny Sunday in mid-

▲ *A major league crowd at a Jones Beach softball game.*

summer will still draw 140,000 to 180,000 people, but it is the special events—the Air Show on Memorial Day, the fireworks display on July 4— that draw the huge crowds these days.

The Great Playground

Many of those who do come here are engaged in something that has been a central part of what might be called the Jones Beach "mission." Back in the 1920s Moses and Al Smith spoke often about the beach as a "healthful" place; that time at the seaside, away from the city airs, would be a restorative, healing experience. From the beginning active play and sports were encouraged and have continued as an integral part of the life of the beach.

"This great playground" is how *Architecture* magazine described the still-new Jones Beach in an article in July 1934, praising its shuffleboard courts, archery range, handball courts, pony track, and a pitch 'n' putt golf course of eighteen holes, as well as its two pools. In addition, group calisthenics classes were held regularly on the beach, and softball was and continues to be played today on two fields.

Ruth Burkert remembers Jones Beach as the great playground of her youth. Burkert, who grew up in Valley Stream, began visiting the beach in the late 1930s. Ruth's father encouraged his only daughter's aquatic abilities, and by age eleven she was able to swim a mile at the West Bathhouse Pool. The regular weekend visits continued during World War II, when her father would walk to the Valley Stream railroad station, rather than drive, during the week, in order to save precious gas-rationing coupons for the weekend. He'd invite the other kids in the neighborhood to come along with them to Jones Beach as well.

"We'd pack up all these kids in my dad's 1939 Chrysler and drive to the beach," she says. "They'd go off and play,

△ *The country's craze for calisthenics continued at the Central Mall in 1937.*

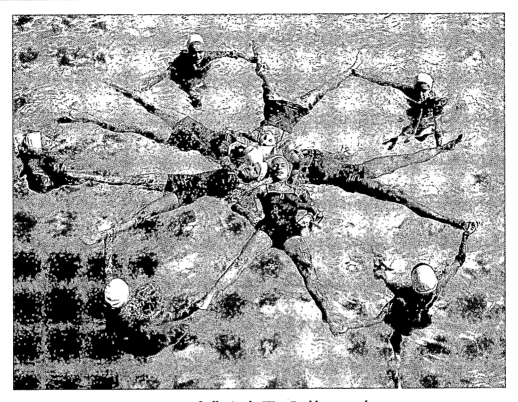

△ *Water ballet in the West Bathhouse pool.*
◁ *The "great playground" in action: While some relax under striped umbrellas (foreground), others join in the calisthenics class—a reminder that vigorous sports and exercise have been an integral part of the Jones Beach experience since its inception.*

but my father would always tell me, 'Do your mile!' When I got that done, I could go play with the other kids."

Ruth started competing on so-called Girls' Days, when young female swimmers raced in the pool. She was good enough that at age sixteen she was recruited to swim in the water ballet—the swim shows held regularly at the West Bathhouse. "Here I was sixteen, seventeen years old, and to have a job where we made good money . . . fifty bucks a week," she says. "I graduated from college and made fifty bucks a week!"

The life of the synchronized swimmer in the Jones Beach water shows was a good one. Ruth and her fellow swimmers arrived at the beach for practice at 8:00 A.M. six days a week. "At noon, we'd be done," she said. Afterward, she would take a calisthenics class, play miniature golf, go shoot bows and arrows at the archery range. "Or we'd go down to the Coast Guard station and they'd take us water skiing," she said.

At night they'd perform their water ballet under the lights of the West Bathhouse. "They were very popular, and they didn't cost anything," she says. "The balcony would always be packed with people."

The water ballets ended when the new Jones Beach Theatre opened in 1952, but Ruth, now seventy-two, can still swim a mile.

Biking the Beach

George A. Murphy may not have been a great swimmer, but he was a great fan of bicycling and of Jones Beach—one who carved a unique place in the sports history of the beach through his enthusiasm and persistence. In 1971 Murphy, a Hempstead town councilman, launched a one-man campaign to build a bicycle route to Jones Beach and to promote bicycling within the state park, which, at that time, was prohibited. "Jones Beach has all the promise of being a bicycle rider's paradise," he wrote in one of the dozens of missives he fired off to state and parks officials, newspapers and community groups in the early 1970s. "[It is] a magical place of fresh air, exhilaration and charm." Murphy waxed poetic in his depiction of Jones Beach, extolling the sea breezes, "delicately salted by nature itself . . . ever present, caressing, pushing, nudging like a child seeking attention . . . sometimes carrying the bicyclist faster than his own leg power, another time testing his endurance and stamina."

Murphy's own stamina seemed endless, as he fought his way through a thicket of naysayers and bureaucratic barriers while galvanizing support from local residents, civic groups, and fellow bicycle enthusiasts.

▲ *Three people with a lifetime of experience at Jones Beach, together on the boardwalk in May,*
2006. All started working here while in high school or college. They are (left to right),
George "Chip" Gorman Jr., director of operations for Long Island State Parks;
Susan Guliani, director of Jones Beach State Park; and John Norbeck, former director of
Jones Beach and former director of Long Island State Parks.

In 1972, to help demonstrate the demand and potential for his bike path, Murphy organized one of the most ambitious participatory sports events in Jones Beach history: a mass ride. Bicyclists would pedal from Merrick Road 5 miles south on the Wantagh Parkway—which officials agreed to close for one day—to the beach, then along the length of the boardwalk. On a crisp, sunny day in late October, 12,000 people turned out for the first Jones Beach Bicycle Jubilee.

"There were no age barriers," reported *Newsday*. "From the tiny tot, asleep in a baby seat, to the senior citizen, they came to ride in their new-found freedom."

Bicycling on the beach's access parkways had been briefly permitted as an experiment during World War II's gas rationing, apparently without much success, and as has often been noted, Jones Beach is designed primarily for automobile access. Whether or not these were reasons for the lukewarm response to Murphy's proposal, it took three more years of letter writing, petitions, and Bicycle Jubilees for his dream to become a reality. But finally, in July 1975, the Jones Beach Bikeway opened. It runs along Wantagh Parkway from Cedar Creek Park in Seaford to the parking lot of the Jones Beach Theatre. Today the 4½-mile path (named in honor of Ellen Farrant, another leader in the local bicycling community) is heavily trafficked not only by bicyclists but also runners, walkers, and in-line skaters. (Bicycles are permitted on the boardwalk as well from October to April.)

By providing, in essence, a third access road to the beach—one relying on muscle as opposed to horsepower—the bike path helped infuse the beach with more active sports participants, who now arrived on two-wheelers instead of sedans. As society became more fitness conscious through the running and fitness booms of the late 1970s and 1980s, activities at the beach began to reflect the change. Shuffleboard was out; bicycling or jogging 5 miles along the boardwalk was in. In May 1984 the new Long Island Half Marathon, a 13.1-mile footrace held in conjunction with the existing full marathon, started at Eisenhower Park and wound its way south before linking up with the Wantagh Parkway at Sunrise Highway. Ten thousand runners made their way south down the parkway to the beach and a scenic finish on the boardwalk. The half marathon would follow that point-to-point course for several years, before logistical problems of getting the runners back to Eisenhower Park after they'd finished caused organizers to reroute it. However, a 5-mile race in June, held as part of a series of Long Island State Park summer races, and a swim/bike/run triathlon in the early fall have both become popular annual fixtures. In addition, an annual September event that attracts about 100 eight-member teams of runners—the Ocean to Sound Relay—starts at Jones Beach and ends 50 miles later at Oyster Bay, symbolically linking the two shores of Long Island. Other fund-raising walkathons and races bring people out by the thousands to the beach as well.

Trump on the Ocean

On a rainy September afternoon in 2006, the name of the man who built Jones Beach was invoked yet again. "It's a Robert Moses kind of day," said Parks Commissioner Castro, addressing a crowd of reporters, cameramen, parks officials, politicians, and other VIPs who filled a tent sent up on the boardwalk.

Castro was referring not to the weather but to the occasion: The announcement of something big, bold, and new at Jones Beach—in this case, a new $30 million restaurant and catering facility on the beach, to be developed by none other than Donald Trump.

To some, the idea of the flamboyant Trump descending on the placid dunes of Jones Beach sounded alarming. After all, this is the man who helped develop Atlantic City—a successful gambling mecca, but exactly the kind of beachfront resort that Moses wanted Jones Beach not to become. Fears were allayed, however, when The Donald himself spoke. "I've been working on this project for fifty-five years," he joked, mentioning that he had visited Jones Beach often as a child. "I know it, I respect it, I love it."

And what he plans to do on it now, he said, is rebuild the Boardwalk restaurant in partnership with restaurateur and catering mogul Steven Carl (himself a native Long Islander who had grown up visiting the beach). The nondescript, modern structure had burned down several years earlier and left an eyesore along the boardwalk. The new luxury restaurant

In September 2006, New York State Parks Commissioner Bernadette Castro introduced real estate titan Donald Trump to announce plans to create "Trump on the Ocean" at Jones Beach, a restaurant and catering facility (artist's rendering shown below).

and catering facility, Trump promises will maintain the architectural integrity of the beach. Sure enough, the artist's rendering shown at the press conference that day depicts a sandstone-colored building that looked like it could have been a third bathhouse.

"When Don said 'Art Deco' Robert Moses had to be smiling," Castro said.

It's an interesting thought. On some levels Moses and Trump couldn't be more different: One a brilliant builder who preferred his deals done behind the scenes and who often didn't trust the private sector; the other, a brash entrepreneur who celebrated what he called *The Art of the Deal* in a best-selling book. Trump has a sense of humor and seems used to being lampooned as well as idolized. It's hard to imagine the serious, thin-skinned Moses ever appearing as a guest on *Saturday Night Live*, much less his own TV reality show.

Still, Moses was and Trump is a big dreamer. And while criticisms immediately rose over the deal—Why wasn't he paying more taxes on his investment? Will the average person be able to get into the new restaurant wearing sandals? What happens if he tries to develop the entire shore-front?—the announcement of "Trump on the Ocean" (scheduled to open in 2008) brought something to Jones Beach rarely seen here in the last few decades: excitement. Trump is the first genuine celebrity to plant roots here since Guy Lombardo a half century ago. And as someone who seems to understand and respect the legacy of the place, he may very well bring attention and a dollop of that valuable but hard-to-define twenty-first-century currency—buzz—to a place that seems to have fallen off the radar screen for some people.

"I'm in love with Jones Beach," Trump said, at the end of the press conference—a comment that on this or any other day, Robert Moses would certainly have had no quarrel with.

The Sporting Life

Back in 2000, a reporter for *Newsday* spent ten hours at Jones Beach to chronicle a day in its "sporting life." Arriving at 6:00 A.M., I found the boardwalk already alive with runners and walkers. Many of them were seniors whose gathering place is Field Six, the eastern end of the board-walk. "We come in rain and snow," said Orrin Smith of North Bellmore, age seventy-three. "And on days we can't walk, we sit, have coffee, and set-tle all the problems of Long Island."

By 8:30, Douglas Sanchez of Freeport was well into his workout on the beach. Sanchez, a native of El Salvador, is a former competitive soccer player who said he still kept in shape by coming here four days a week and kicking a soccer ball back and forth for 2 miles along the beach. "There's no beach like Jones Beach," he said.

Jones Beach is still a popular tourist destination, and on this day one tourist was Eleanor Rahim, a Londoner visiting the beach during a busi-ness trip to New York. The first time she saw it, she told the reporter, "I was amazed. We don't have huge expanses of beach like this in the U.K." Rahim spent the morning at Jones Beach with her friend Charles Miller of Manhattan, enjoying an activity that has been popular here since the 1930s: the pitch 'n' putt golf course (15,000 to 18,000 rounds of golf are played annually on this eighteen-hole course).

Not all the activity at Jones Beach State Park is centered on the boardwalk. That Memorial Day weekend in 2000, Derrick and Joanna Nipcon traversed the Jones Beach bike path on in-line skates and bicycle, respectively, arriving at the terminus of the path. "We used to live in the countryside," said Derrick, who emigrated here from Poland with Joanna seven years ago. "We were used to a lot of green. Here, we can feel nature again."

Nature gets even closer at the Field Ten fishing piers. Like the walkers, the fishermen are here all year long. They come morning, noon, and night, depending on the tides. They catch fluke, flounder, and striped bass. And they all seemed to defer to the man known as Zorba the Greek, John Zorbagallis: a vigorous, at the time eighty-three-year-old from Bellmore, who had been fishing here for more than fifty years and was one of the few still at the beach who had actually met Robert Moses. That happened during the opening of the fishing piers a half century earlier. "I gave his wife a bunch of striped bass," he says. "She gave me a bottle of Southern Comfort."

There were more sports and sportspeople that day, partaking in what then-superintendent Frank Kollar called "the outdoor experience" that is Jones Beach: surfcasters on the jetty, basketball players on the court, pickup football players on the sands, softball players on the fields, boaters on the channel—not to mention a brave swimmer or two in the cold early-season water. Meanwhile, a steady, seemingly endless stream of walkers and runners continued along the boardwalk.

It seemed to this reporter that almost all of the 19,000 visitors that day were involved in some form of sports activity. It's a safe bet that few of them knew much about the history of Jones Beach, but if they had, they—just like all visitors to Jones Beach—might have seconded the fervently expressed opinions of Zorbagallis. "God bless Robert Moses," he said. "Whatever other faults he may have had, what he did here was unbelievable."

Moses died in July 1981 at age ninety-two—almost sixty years after the day that he first set foot on the raw, inaccessible beach named after Pirate Jones and had his inspired vision of the greatest public waterfront facility in the world. His vision became a reality. And while the King of

All Beaches has changed—fields have come and gone, buildings razed and restored—its noble heart remains unchanged, its grandeur unabated (in some cases, such as the beautiful, reclaimed-by-nature West End, even enhanced). "Jones Beach remains the finest beach I have ever seen, finer than the exclusive resorts on the Caribbean, finer than the private beaches in Malibu," wrote historian Doris Kearns Goodwin in her 1997 memoir of growing up on Long Island, *Wait Till Next Year.* It remains, she said, "a paradise for adults and children alike."

The man who created it remained both proud and defensive. During an interview in the 1970s with *Newsday*'s Tom Morris, he pounded a fist on his desk, swiveled his chair to face the reporter, and wagged a finger in his face to emphasize a point. "Listen to me, chum," Moses said, according to Morris's written recollections. "These ecologists are Johnny-come-latelys. In my day, we called it 'conservation.' At Jones Beach, if we waited for the environment enthusiasts the whole goddamn place would be covered with small cottages right now."

Given the patterns of development on Long Island in the last three decades, it's quite likely that if Moses had not come along, Jones Beach today would be covered with McMansions and luxury condo developments, almost certainly inaccessible to the general public. Without his efforts in the early twentieth century to win the land for the public, the bay, the dunes, and the wildlife of the West End might not be protected today in the twenty-first. The old fisherman Zorbagallis was right. Whatever his faults, Robert Moses gave us Jones Beach.

It's a jewel.

Acknowledgments

This book was Phyllis Singer's idea. It began in 2004, when I was a contributing writer on a summer-long series published by *Newsday* on the seventy-fifth anniversary of Jones Beach. At the time, Phyllis was assistant managing editor. Later, as a freelance acquisitions editor for the Globe Pequot Press, Phyllis thought to put the whole story of Jones Beach between two covers. Readers will be the judge, but I think they will see that Phyllis, as so often is the case, was right: Jones Beach is a great story, an important story, and one never fully told in book form until now.

The people at Long Island State Parks—which administrates Jones Beach—are justifiably proud of their crown jewel, and were eager to see it done justice. First among them is the former "Mayor" of Jones Beach and later director of Long Island State Parks, John Norbeck, who spent most of his life and career working for parks, and who loves and knows Jones Beach like few others. His two long-time colleagues, director of operations George "Chip" Gorman and current Jones Beach director Sue Guliani, made important contributions to this book, as well—not the least of which was their patient and cheerful responses to our questions and requests. Many others on the Parks staff got involved in this book, and each was a pleasure to work with: My friend Peggy Kucija, Sue Precker, Bob Harrison, John Dileo, and Anne-Marie Agostinello all deserve special thanks.

Bernadette Castro, the Commissioner of New York State Parks, Recreation and Historic Preservation, was as animated and entertaining in our interviews for this book as she is on the Don Imus WFAN radio show in New York, where she has been a frequent guest over the years. We thank Bernadette and her able assistant Lorri DeRossi for their help.

An illustrated history cannot happen without illustrations—which in the case of this book are primarily the marvelous photos from the New York State Parks archives. Our thanks to the folks in Albany who helped get us these terrific photos: James Gold, Director, Bureau of Historic Sites; Anne R. Cassidy, Collections Manager, Bureau of Historic Sites; and Assistant Archivists Mary Klimack and Hajime Stickel.

To supplement these photos, we employed the services of the consummate Jones Beach photographer, my long-time friend and *Newsday* colleague Dan Goodrich; and the aforementioned Bill Powell, whose family has worked the waters off the beach for generations, and who contributed some of his art, memorabilia, and family photos.

At Globe Pequot we thank Mary Norris, our editor, for believing in the project and for her astute suggestions on the structure of the book, and Amy Paradysz, our efficient project editor. My agent Linda Konner provided wise counsel, as well, but there's nothing new there: She usually does. I would also like to thank others who served as sounding boards, in particular good friends Bob Spina Jr., Fran Ricigliano, and Peter Sikowitz.

At New York Institute of Technology, where I teach writing and journalism, my work on this book was supported by an Institutional Support of Research and Creativity (ISRC) grant. I thank the members of the grant committee, as well as NYIT administration and faculty colleagues alike for their ongoing interest in and encouragement of my writing.

Parts of this book originated in *Newsday* stories I have done over the years, and for those I thank the various editors who helped guide them to fruition. We also thank one of those editors, Harvey Aronson, who was born the same year as Jones Beach State Park, for his precious and beautifully written memories of Jones Beach, some of which are included in this book. Thanks also to long-time Long Island columnist and personality Ed Lowe for his wonderful introduction to the book.

Geri Solomon, assistant Dean of Special Collections at the Long Island Studies Institute of Hofstra University—home to an extensive and valuable collection of Jones Beach and Robert Moses-related materials—was a wonderful guide to her collections, as were the members of her staff. Also thanks to Valerie Wingfield at the Robert Moses papers of the New York Public Library, which provided valuable background information on the man who built the beach. Ed Smits, former Nassau County historian, was a helpful guide and sounding board. His comprehensive history of Nassau County, *Suburbia USA,* was also a very useful source.

For our chapter on the amazing Thomas Jones: Lillian Bryson and Ken Noelsch of the DeLancey Floyd-Jones Free Library; Gail Klubnick of the Historical Society of the Massapequas; Thomas Kuehhas and Stacie Hammond of the Oyster Bay Historical Society; and Christine Kinealy, professor of history at the University of Central Lancashire, UK, all provided important information that helped us recreate his shadowy life and the turbulent era in which he lived.

For insight into Jones Beach pre-1929 and the High Hill Beach colony: The aforementioned Bill Powell and Ben Sohm—the last of the South Shore baymen—and their friends and protégés Ken and Matt Bernstein, Matt Sohm and Ray Sullivan, brought me out on the South Oyster Bay on two memorable trips, and in the process taught me a great deal about life on the water in the years preceding Jones Beach and about the ecology of the beach and the bay, as well. Frank Scarangella and his West Gilgo Beach neighbors Nate and Carol Bard shared with me knowledge and materials relating to the history of High Hill Beach, as did historian Josh Soren, who probably knows more about this long-lost beach colony than anyone.

"Specialist" knowledge on a wide range of topics was necessary for various aspects of the beach. So we thank Douglas Flood, Guy Enroughty, and the late Chris Doty for their help on better understanding the life, career, and music of Guy Lombardo; John Galluzzo, executive director of the U.S. Life-Saving Heritage Association, for lending his expertise on the history of the U.S. Life Saving Service; George Marth, Ed Peters, Jay Lieberfarb, and Joe Scalise for teaching me a little about what it's like to be a lifeguard at Jones Beach; and the webmasters at www.jblifeguard.com for a good source of information. Also, thanks to Steve Branch of the Audiovisual Department of the Reagan National Library for helping secure a copy of the Reagan's movie *The Girl From Jones Beach,* and Lauren Gilbert, arts librarian at the New York Institute of Technology, for locating a copy of the 1934 *Architecture* magazine about the beach. Marjorie Weinberg, whose loving tribute to her mentor Rosebud Yellow Robe is cited in the bibliography, was a big help and supporter of the book. I thank her, as I do all of the friends and acquaintances (too numerous to mention) who shared their own Jones Beach memories—many of them are included in the book.

Finally, to my mother Dolores who hates the beach but loves her son, my ever-supportive wife Donna and my ten-year-old son Andrew, who found Jones Beach not nearly as interesting as the Blue Angels who flew overhead and the NASCAR vehicles on display along the boardwalk, but who may someday feel differently. And to my dad and grandfather, John and Josef Hanc, who appreciated Jones Beach the way that only those who come from a place where there are no oceans or unlimited vistas really can—and who, I like to think, would have enjoyed this book.

Since they no longer can, I hope you have.

Bibliography

Periodicals

Long Island Forum

Long Island Press

Nassau Democrat-Review

Newsday

New York Herald-Tribune

The New York Times

Collections

DeLancey Floyd-Jones Free Library

Long Island Studies Institute of Hofstra University

New York State Office of Parks, Recreation and Historic Preservation,
    Long Island Regional Headquarters

Robert Moses Papers, Manuscripts and Archives Division of the New
    York Public Library

Ronald Reagan Presidential Library

Books

Badger, Anthony J. *The New Deal: The Depression Years 1933–40*. New
    York: Macmillan, 1989.

Blakelock, Chester R. *History of the Long Island State Parks*. Amityville, N.Y.: Long Island Forum (Permission of the Lewis Historical Publishing Co.), 1959.

Cahn, Ira. *An Illustrated History of Massapequa*. Massapequa, N.Y.: Massapequa Publishing, 1961.

Caro, Robert. *The Power Broker: Robert Moses and the Fall of New York*. New York: Albert A. Knopf, 1974.

Cordingly, David. *Under the Black Flag: The Romance and the Reality of Life Among the Pirates*. New York: Random House, 1995.

de L. Landon, Michael *Erin and Britannia: The Historical Background to a Modern Tragedy*. Chicago: Nelson-Hall, 1981.

Finan, Christopher. *Alfred E. Smith: The Happy Warrior*. New York: Hill and Wang, 2002.

Flint, Martha Bockee. *Long Island Before the Revolution: A Colonial Study*. Port Washington, N.Y.: Ira J. Friedman, Inc., 1967.

Floyd-Jones, Thomas. *Thomas Jones and His Descendants: The Floyd-Jones Families*. New York: J. Grant Senia Press, 1906.

Fry, Peter, and Fiona Somerset Fry. *A History of Ireland*. New York: Barnes & Noble Books, 1993.

Gabriel, Ralph Henry. *The Evolution of Long Island: A Story of Land and Sea*. Port Washington, N.Y.: Ira J. Friedman, Inc., 1960.

Goodwin, Doris Kearns. *Wait Till Next Year: A Memoir*. New York: Simon & Schuster, 1997.

Jones, John H. *The Jones Family of Long Island*. New York: Tobias A. Wright, 1907.

Lencek, Lena, and Gideon Bosker. *The Beach: The History of Paradise on Earth*. New York: Viking, 1998.

Lombardo, Guy with Jack Altshul. *Auld Acquaintance*. Garden City, N.Y.: Doubleday & Company, Inc., 1975.

Long Island Studies Institute (Joann Krieg, editor). *Robert Moses: Single-Minded Genius*. Interlaken, N.Y.: Empire State Books/Heart of the Lakes Publishing, 1989.

Murphy, George A. *A Dream Come True: A Documented History of the Jones Beach Bikeway* (unpublished).

Smits, Edward. *Nassau: Suburbia, USA*. Syosset, N.Y.: Friends of the Nassau County Museum, 1974.

Thompson, B. F. *History of Long Island*. Port Washington, N.Y.: Ira J. Friedman, Inc., 1962.

Watkins, T. H. *The Great Depression*. Boston: Little, Brown & Company, 1993.

Wecter, Dixon. *The Age of the Great Depression*. New York: The MacMillan Company, 1948.

Weeks, George L. Jr. *Isle of Shells (Long Island)*. Islip, N.Y.: Buys Bros., 1965.

Weinberg, Marjorie. *The Real Rosebud: The Triumph of a Lakota Woman*. Lincoln, Neb.: University of Nebraska Press, 2004.

Index

John Hanc is a writer specializing in active and outdoor sports, fitness, and history. A long-time contributing writer for Long Island, New York-based *Newsday*, Hanc's work has also appeared in such publications as *AARP Bulletin*, *Boston Globe Sunday Magazine, Men's Fitness, Men's Health, New York Times, Runner's World, Reader's Digest, Smithsonian* and *Yoga Journal*. An associate professor of journalism at the New York Institute of Technology in Old Westbury, New York, he is also the author of six previous books.

About the New York State Parks Archives

New York State Parks manages, preserves, and protects the nation's oldest and most comprehensive system of scenic and historic properties, from Montauk to Niagara Falls. The institutional records of the Long Island Region represent a unique resource, one that documents the design, development, management, and public use of state park lands from the 1920s to the present day.

Staff from New York State Parks' Bureau of Historic Sites have examined, catalogued, and re-housed over 80,000 photographic negatives and 25,000 photographic prints documenting the Robert Moses legacy on Long Island. An additional 100,000 architectural and engineering drawings that document the region's parks and parkways infrastructure are also being archivally processed, to ensure their long-term preservation.

Together, these photographic materials and drawings constitute the Long Island Regional Archive. The Archive, which is housed in a handsome ca. 1920 brick farm building known as the "Hay Barn" at Planting Fields Arboretum State Historic Park in Oyster Bay, is a state-of-the-art archival storage and research facility. The Archive is of value not only to State Parks staff but also to urban and social historians, urban-, recreation-, and land-planners, environmentalists, and others who share an interest in the history of one of our country's most significant park systems.

For more information, visit www.nysparks.com.